WORLDCOMP'13
July 22-25, 2013
Las Vegas Nevada, USA
www.world-academy-of-science.org

PROCEEDINGS OF THE 2013 INTERNATIONAL CONFERENCE ON SEMANTIC WEB & WEB SERVICES

SWWS 2013

Editors

Hamid R. Arabnia
Leonidas Deligiannidis
Ashu M. G. Solo
Fernando G. Tinetti

FIREWALL MEDIA
(An Imprint of Laxmi Publications Pvt. Ltd.)
An ISO 9001:2008 Company
BENGALURU • CHENNAI • COCHIN • GUWAHATI • HYDERABAD
JALANDHAR • KOLKATA • LUCKNOW • MUMBAI • RANCHI • NEW DELHI
BOSTON (USA) • ACCRA (GHANA) • NAIROBI (KENYA)

This volume contains papers presented at The 2013 International Conference on Semantic Web & Web Services (SWWS'13). Their inclusion in this publication does not necessarily constitute endorsements by editors or by the publisher.

Branches		
Bengaluru	080-26 75 69 30	
Chennai	044-24 34 47 26,	24 35 95 07
Cochin	0484-237 70 04,	405 13 03
Guwahati	0361-254 36 69,	251 38 81
Hyderabad	040-27 55 53 83,	27 55 53 93
Jalandhar	0181-222 12 72	
Kolkata	033-22 27 43 84	
Lucknow	0522-220 99 16	
Mumbai	022-24 91 54 15,	24 92 78 69
Ranchi	0651-220 44 64	

PUBLISHED IN INDIA BY

FIREWALL MEDIA
(An Imprint of Laxmi Publications Pvt. Ltd.)

An ISO 9001:2008 Company
113, GOLDEN HOUSE, DARYAGANJ,
NEW DELHI - 110002, INDIA
Telephone : 91-11-4353 2500, 4353 2501
Fax : 91-11-2325 2572, 4353 2528
www.laxmipublications.com info@laxmipublications.com

C—
Printed at Repro Knowledgecast Limited, Thane

Foreword

It gives us great pleasure to introduce this collection of papers to be presented at the 2013 International Conference on Semantic Web and Web Services (SWWS'13), July 22 through 25, 2013, at The New Tropicana Hotel, Las Vegas, USA.

An important mission of the World Congress in Computer Science, Computer Engineering, and Applied Computing (a federated congress to which this conference is affiliated with) includes *"Providing a unique platform for a diverse community of constituents composed of scholars, researchers, developers, educators, and practitioners. The Congress makes concerted effort to reach out to participants affiliated with diverse entities (such as: universities, institutions, corporations, government agencies, and research centers/labs) from all over the world. The congress also attempts to connect participants from institutions that have **teaching** as their main mission with those who are affiliated with institutions that have **research** as their main mission. The congress uses a quota system to achieve its institution and geography diversity objectives."* By any definition of diversity, this congress is among the most diverse scientific meeting in USA. We are proud to report that this federated congress has authors and participants from 82 different nations representing variety of personal and scientific experiences that arise from differences in culture and values. As can be seen (see below), the program committee of this conference as well as the program committee of all other tracks of the federated congress are as diverse as its authors and participants.

The program committee would like to thank all those who submitted papers for consideration. Each submitted paper was peer-reviewed by two experts in the field for originality, significance, clarity, impact, and soundness. In cases of contradictory recommendations, a member of the conference program committee was charged to make the final decision; often, this involved seeking help from additional referees. In addition, papers whose authors included a member of the conference program committee were evaluated using the double-blinded review process. One exception to the above evaluation process was for papers that were submitted directly to chairs/organizers of pre-approved sessions/workshops; in these cases, the chairs/organizers were responsible for the evaluation of such submissions. The overall paper acceptance rate for regular papers was 31%; 9% of the remaining papers were accepted as poster papers (at the time of this writing, we had not yet received the acceptance rate for a few individual tracks.)

We are very grateful to the many colleagues who offered their services in organizing the conference. In particular, we would like to thank the members of the Program Committee of SWWS'13, members of the congress Steering Committee, and members of the committees of federated congress tracks that have topics within the scope of SWWS. Many individuals listed below, will be requested after the conference to provide their expertise and services for selecting papers for publication (extended versions) in journal special issues as well as for publication in a set of research books (to be prepared for publishers including: Springer, Elsevier, BMC, and others).

- *Prof. Babak Akhgar (World Congress Steering Committee); Fellow of the British Computer Society, CITP; Professor of Informatics; Co-Director of CENTRIC (Centre of Excellence in Terrorism, Resilience, Intelligence & organised Crime research), Sheffield Hallam University, Sheffield, UK*
- *Dr. Fahad Al-Harby (EEE); The National Centre for Financial & Economic Information, Ministry of Finance, Riyadh, Saudi Arabia*
- *Prof. Nizar Al-Holou (World Congress Steering Committee); Professor and Chair, Electrical and Computer Engineering Department; Vice Chair, IEEE/SEM-Computer Chapter; University of Detroit Mercy, Detroit, Michigan, USA*
- *Prof. Hamid R. Arabnia (World Congress Steering Committee); Professor, Computer Science; Editor-in-Chief, The Journal of Supercomputing (Springer); Elected Fellow, Int'l Society of Intelligent Biological Medicine (ISIBM); The University of Georgia, Department of Computer Science, USA*
- *Prof. Ezendu Ariwa (Publicity Vice-Chair); Chair, IEEE Consumer Electronics Chapter, UK&RI; Visiting Professor, Gulf University, Bahrain*
- *Dr. Azita Bahrami (Session Chair, EEE + Session Chair, FECS); President, IT Consult, USA*
- *Prof. Juan Cuadrado-Gallego; Universidad de Alcala, Edificio Politecnico, Madrid, Spain; Ecole de technologie superieure, University of Quebec, Canada*
- *Prof. Leonidas Deligiannidis; Professor, Computer Science, Wentworth Institute of Technology, MA, USA*

- *Somdip Dey (ICOMP); St. Xavier's College (Autonomous), Kolkata, India*
- *Prof. George A. Gravvanis (Vice Chair of GCA); Democritus University of Thrace, Greece*
- *Dr. K. S. S. Iyer (PDPTA); Symbiosis Institute of Telecom Management, Pune, India*
- *Prof. George Jandieri (World Congress Steering Committee); Georgian Technical University, Tbilisi, Georgia; Chief Scientist, The Institute of Cybernetics, Georgian Academy of Science, Georgia; Editorial Board Member: International Journal of Microwaves and Optical Technology, Georgia*
- *Prof. Seifedine Kadry (PDPTA); School of Engineering, American University of the Middle East, Kuwait*
- *Prof. Dattatraya V. Kodavade (World Congress Steering Committee); Head of Computer Science and Engineering, D.K.T.E Society's Textile & Engineering Institute, Ichalkaranji, Maharashtra State, India*
- *Prof. B. Raja Sarath Kumar; Principal, Lenora College of Engineering, Andhra Pradesh, India*
- *Prof. Kun Chang Lee (World Congress Steering Committee); Prof. of MIS and WCU Prof. of Creativity Science, Business School & Department of Interaction Science, Sungkyunkwan University, South Korea*
- *Dr. Bala Krishna Maddali (GCA); University School of Information Technology, GGS Indraprastha University, New Delhi, India*
- *Muhammad Naufal Bin Mansor; Intelligent Signal Processing Group (ISP), University Malaysia Perlis, Kangar, Perlis, Malaysia*
- *Arshad Mansoor; Pakistan Aeronautical Complex, Pakistan*
- *Prof. George Markowsky (World Congress Steering Committee); Professor and Associate Director, School of Computing and Information Science; Chair International Advisory Board of IEEE IDAACS; Director 2013 Northeast Collegiate Cyber Defense Competition; Cooperating Professor School of Policy & International Affairs UMaine; University of Maine, Orono, Maine, USA*
- *Dr. Sara Moein; Editorial Board, International Journal of Science and Technology; Faculty of Engineering, MultiMedia University, Malaysia*
- *Dr. Ali Mostafaeipour; Industrial Engineering Department, Yazd University, Iran*
- *Dr. Saurabh Mukherjee; Associate Professor, Department of Computer Science, Banasthali University, Banasthali, Rajasthan, India*
- *Dr. Asoke Nath (EEE + FCS), Department of Computer Science, St. Xavier's College, India*
- *Prof. G. N. Pandey (World Congress Steering Committee); Vice-Chancellor, Arunachal University of Studies, Arunachal Pradesh, India; Adjunct Prof., Indian Institute of Information Technology, India*
- *Prof. James J. (Jong Hyuk) Park (World Congress Steering Committee); Professor of Computer Science and Engineering, Seoul National University of Science and Technology (SeoulTech), Korea; President, KITCS; President, FTRA; Editor-in-Chiefs: HCIS, JoC and IJITCC Journals*
- *Dr. Satish Penmatsa; University of Maryland - Eastern Shore, Maryland, USA*
- *Prof. Junfeng Qu; Clayton State University, Morrow, Georgia, USA*
- *Prof. B. V. A. N. S. S. Prabhakar Rao (ICAI); School of Computing Science and Engineering, VIT University, Chennai Campus, India*
- *Dr. Liang Shi; Senior Researcher, McAfee, USA*
- *Ashu M. G. Solo, (Publicity Chair); Fellow of British Computer Society, Principal/R&D Engineer, Maverick Technologies America Inc., USA*
- *Prof. Fernando G. Tinetti (World Congress Steering Committee); School of CS, Universidad Nacional de La Plata, La Plata, Argentina; Co-editor, Journal of Computer Science and Technology (JCS&T)*
- *Dr. Predrag Tosic (World Congress Steering Committee); Microsoft, Washington, USA*
- *Prof. Vladimir Volkov (World Congress Steering Committee & Vice-Chair of IPCV); The Bonch-Bruevich State University of Telecommunications, Saint-Petersburg, Russia*
- *Dr. Wei Wei (ICOMP); School of CS and Engineering, Xi'an University of Technology, Xi'an, P. R. China*
- *Dr. Alexander Wohrer (ICOMP + GCA); Program Manager ICT at Vienna Science and Technology Fund, Schlickgasse, Vienna, Austria*
- *Prof. Jongwook Woo; Director, High-Performance Information Computing Center (HiPiC), Computer Information Systems Department, California State University, Los Angeles, California, USA*

As Sponsors-at-large, partners, and/or organizers each of the followings (separated by semicolons) provided help for at least one track of the World Congress: Aldebaran Robotics Inc., USA (http://www.aldebaran-robotics.com); Altera Corporation, USA (http://www.altera.com/); Computer Science Research, Education, and Applications Press (CSREA); Impulse Accelerated Technologies, Inc., USA (http://www.impulseaccelerated.com/); NVIDIA Corporation, USA (http://www.nvidia.com/object/about-nvidia.html); Parallella Community, Supercomputing for Everyone, USA (http://forums.parallella.org/); Pico Computing, Inc., USA (http://picocomputing.com/); SemiWiki.com, The Semiconductor Wiki Project, USA (http://www.semiwiki.com/); Solarflare Communications, Inc., USA (http://www.solarflare.com/); Stream Computing, Performance Engineers, The

Netherlands (http://streamcomputing.eu/); Taylor & Francis, UK (http://www.taylorandfrancis.com/); US Chapter of World Academy of Science (http://www.world-academy-of-science.org/) ; and WEBestSOL & Webest Solutions Ltd, UK (http://webestsol.com/). In addition, a number of university faculty members and their staff (names appear on the cover of the set of proceedings), several publishers of computer science and computer engineering books and journals, chapters and/or task forces of computer science associations/organizations from 5 countries, and developers of high-performance machines and systems provided significant help in organizing the conference as well as providing some resources. We are grateful to them all.

We express our gratitude to keynote, invited, and individual conference/tracks and tutorial speakers - the list of speakers appears on the conference web site. We would also like to thank the followings: UCMSS (Universal Conference Management Systems & Support, California, USA) for managing all aspects of the conference; Dr. Tim Field of APC for managing the printing of the proceedings; and the staff of the New Tropicana Hotel in Las Vegas for the professional service they provided. Last but not least, we would like to thank the Co-Editors of SWWS'13: Prof. Hamid R. Arabnia, Prof. Leonidas Deligiannidis, Ashu M. G. Solo, and Prof. Fernando G. Tinetti.

We present the proceedings of SWWS'13.

Steering Committee, 2013
http://www.world-academy-of-science.org/

Contents

SESSION: WEB SERVICES AND APPLICATIONS

SESSION: SEMANTIC WEB

SESSION: ONTOLOGIES

SESSION: POSTERS AND SHORT PAPERS

SESSION: BIOINFORMATICS

SESSION

WEB SERVICES AND APPLICATIONS

Chair(s)

TBA

Integrating Declarative Processes and SOA: A Declarative Web Service Orchestrator

Natália Silva[1,2], **Renata Carvalho**[1], **Ricardo Lima**[1], **and Cesar Oliveira**[1]
[1]Center of Informatics, Federal University of Pernambuco, Recife, Pernambuco, Brazil
[2]C.E.S.A.R - Recife Center for Advanced Studies and Systems, Recife, Pernambuco, Brazil
Email: {ncs, rwm, rmfl, calo}@cin.ufpe.br

Abstract—*Service Oriented Architecture (SOA) is a computer model that aims at building new software by assembling independent and loosely coupled services. Traditional web service orchestration is a mechanism for combining and coordinating different web services based on a predefined pattern. However the orchestration requirements may evolve due to business needs. In business context, the declarative approach has emerged to provide flexibility by modeling* what *must be done but not* how *it must be executed through business rules. When working with such a model, the results produced depend on the users' preferences. It is therefore fundamental that orchestration mechanisms provide simple yet efficient ways to dynamically make service composition. This paper proposes a web service orchestrator for declarative processes that makes service composition at runtime. The resulting business process obey all the business rules. The composition is done as the user chooses the service to run, providing an application-aligned infrastructure that can be scaled based on the needs of each business process, since it is described using declarative strategy.*

Keywords: Service Oriented Architecture, runtime orchestration, flexible process, dynamic service composition.

1. Introduction

Service Oriented Architecture (SOA) is a software architecture that focuses on delivering functionalities through services that can be reused across an enterprise. However these services are independent, they are defined in sequences to fulfill business processes. Services operate without any context from other processes within the organization.

Not only can SOA deliver on its promises of reusability and ability (usefulness), but it can also reduce the overall cost of ownership through the standards-based approach (ease of use) [1]. Moreover, SOA provides a complete integration between data and application.

Web services are an established technology for implementing SOA. They can be composed to create a higher level services or applications. Through service composition a complex service can be created by aggregating component services available. Conventionally, the web service composition specifies what services need to be invoked, in what order, and how to handle exceptional conditions [2]. Standard interfaces (such as WSDL), protocols (such as SOAP) for describing and invoking web services, and the loose-coupling of these services are important characteristics that lead to more interoperable distributed systems [3].

The SOA orchestration mechanism uses a central process to control the execution of web services. It receives the client requests and invokes the component services. This mechanism is referred as a centralized orchestration [4].

The orchestrator behavior may evolve as the business requirements change. Hence, several approaches emerged to provide more flexibility to business process execution [5]. The declarative approach provides the desired flexibility by modeling *what* must be done but not *how* it must be executed [6]. When working with such a model, users are driven by the system to produce required results. However, the manner in which results are produced depends on the usersÕ decisions along the process execution. Since the orchestrator behavior changes whenever the user invokes a service execution, it is important to provide a simple and efficient way to modify the services composition dynamically.

This paper proposes an orchestration mechanism that makes the service composition at runtime. Instead of binding pre-modeled compositions, the proposed flexible orchestrator binds the output data of a service to the input data of another service at runtime. The composition is done as the user chooses the service to run, following a declarative approach for the business process. For the automated arrangement, coordination, management, and binding of services, the user must provide some data configuration through an intuitive XML file. Our orchestrator provides an application-aligned infrastructure that can generate various web service composition at runtime based on the needs of each business process, since it is described using the declarative strategy.

The remainder of the paper is organized as follows. We first introduce the concept of flexible process in Section 2. Some related works and their main contributions are compared to this work in Section 3. Section 4 presents our web-service orchestrator. The section shows the benefits provided by our orchestrator and details its architecture. Section 5 conducts a case study. Finally, Section 6 discuss the main conclusions we draw in this paper.

2. Flexible Processes

When the company tasks are less repetitive and predictable, workflows are not able to properly represent the possible flows of work [5]. They often are either too simple, thus unable to handle the variety of situations that occur; or they are too complex, trying to model every imagined possible situation but being hard to maintain. In both cases they may cause several problems to the company. To tackle these problems, flexible processes surged as a shift paradigm from traditional approaches [7]. The word *flexible* in this context means the process is not static, it can change or get adjusted during its execution according to different situations.

Several different implementations of tool support for managing enterprises employing flexible processes have been proposed. They can be split into two categories:

- *change-oriented*: allow the business process change at runtime;
- *declarative*: less prescriptive than workflow; it adopts declarative languages.

This paper focuses on declarative process, whose the main concept is to define the business process behavior by business rules described through a declarative language. Traditional workflows take an "inside-to-outside" strategy, where all the executions alternatives must be detailed on the process model. On the other hand, a declarative process takes an "outsite-to-inside" strategy, where the execution options are guided by constraints [8]. Adding new constraints reduces the number of execution options.

In this constraint-based approach, a process model is composed of two elements: activities and constraints. An activity is an action that updates the enterprise status and is executed by a resource. A constraint is a business rule which must be respected during the whole process execution. Thereby, the permission to execute activities is controlled by business rules, where each activity is enabled to be executed as soon as the business rules allow it.

3. Related Works

There are some tools available to support the execution of declarative processes [9] [10] [11] [12]. However none of them employs Service Oriented Computing (SOC) concepts. In all these systems, the activities are not actually executed by the tool . The user only informs when he starts and conclude/cancel each activity but its execution is not integrated to the system. The user has to manually execute the activities.

Current web service solutions are not able to execute flexible processes because their implementations provide a static execution [13]. BPEL [14], the facto standard for web services business process description, is static and not easy to adapt [15]. Hence, there is a need for service oriented solutions to be more flexible since the business policies and environments change quickly. In this context, some solutions [16][17] [18] [19] [20][21] employs SOC and intends to make BPEL descriptions more flexible or adaptable.

These solutions makes the BPEL more adaptive by allowing dynamic composition. The idea is to make the service composition during runtime. This is less prescriptive than the traditional static composition strategy. Some works [16][17] aims at improving the QoS and prevent SLA violations. They keep the composition structure and monitor the QoS parameters to decide which service to invoke from a group of possible services.

Other dynamic composition solutions [18] [19] [20][21] adapt the business process structure to reflect the current status of the process execution. Such approaches do not redeploy the process after modifying their structure.

VxBPEL [18] is an extension to the standard BPEL language that provides VariationPoint. VariationPoint is a container of possible BPEL codes available for selection at runtime.

AO4BPEL [19]is another extension that improves the business process flexibility using aspect-oriented concepts. The BPEL structure can be changed through the aspects defined. The user can activate the aspects during runtime and then the web service flow composition can change at runtime. CEVICHE [20] is a tool that employs the AO4BPEL. CEVICHEÕs users do not activate the aspects. Instead, it activates the aspects through a Complex Event Processing (CEP) engine. CEVICHE can automatically decide *when* and *how* to adapt the system by analyzing events with CEP technology.

Xiao *et al.* [21] proposes a constraint-based framework that employs process fragments. A process fragment is a portion of a process that can be reused across multiple processes. These fragments are selected and composed based on some business constraints and policies. The resulting process is a standard BPEL process, deployable on standard BPEL engines.

Another dynamic composition proposal is the SCENE service execution environment [22]. It allows the BPEL to be changed at runtime by choosing the correct service to be invoked based on business rules. These rules are used to realize the correct bindings between the BPEL engine and the services. For this purpose, there is a rule engine that makes the decisions about the services selection.

All the aforementioned works are extensions to BPEL aiming at making it more adaptive. However, none of them provide ways to execute declarative processes. Since declarative processes do not have any predefined structured, it is not possible to execute them using BPEL or its extensions.

4. A declarative Web-service orchestrator

In the absence of solutions to execute declarative business processes through web services composition, we propose a flexible orchestrator. Our work aims at allowing users to compose services at runtime, generating a business process that respect the business rules. As in declarative processes, if the business rules do not prohibit the execution of an activity, it is enabled. The user chooses one of the enabled activities (service operation) to execute, generating a state transition. Then, the engine evaluates the process rules to determine the set of enabled transition in the next state.

To implement the orchestration mechanism, the engine must register the input/output data of the services executed. The current implementation supports values of the following types: int, float, double, String, or boolean types, or a list of any of these types.

This section presents our declarative orchestration mechanism and the architecture of our solution.

4.1 Process Definition

Before starting the process execution, the user must specify the process activities, their respective service bindings, and the business rules of the business model. Moreover, the user should provide the data bindings necessary for the execution of each activity (service operation). We created a XML-based language to express such business model and service properties. The code in 1 presents an example of a process definition using this language.

```
<process>
  <globalData>
    <variable name="list"
       type="STRING_LIST"></variable>
    <variable name="output" type="INT"
       initialValue="5"></variable>
  </globalData>
  <activities>
    <activity name="activtyA">
      <serviceBinding operation="operationName"
         wsdlUrl="serviceUrl"
         portType="portType"
         binding="binding" />
      <dataInputBinding>
        <variableBinding variableName="list"
           global="true"
           expression="xpath:/input/list" />
        <variableBinding
           variableName="localVariable"
           global="false" type="FLOAT"
           expression="xpath:/input/test" />
      </dataInputBinding>
      <dataOutputBinding>
        <variableBinding variableName="output"
           expression="//servicoResponse/return"
           />
      </dataOutputBinding>
    </activity>
  </activities>
</process>
```

XML 1: Process Definition

The main tag *process* contains all the necessary information to the process execution.The user must specify the activities and the global data the orchestrator will manage. The tags *activities* and *globalData* are used with this propose.

The *globalData* tag contains the list of global variables. These variables are public. Any activity in the process can access and modify their values during its execution. A *variable* tag contains three attributes: *name*, *type*, and *initialValue*. The *name* and *type* are required and refer to the variable name and variable data type respectively. The *initialValue* is optional and indicates the variableÕs initial value.. If it is not defined, the variable is initialized with the default value for its data type.

The *activities* tag contains a list of activities. Each one has only one attribute, that defines its name, and three properties: *serviceBinding*, *dataInputBinding*, and *dataOutputBinding*. The *serviceBinding* tag includes all the necessary information to associate this activity execution with a service invocation. Such information is described through four attributes:: *operation*, *wsdlUrl*, *portType*, and *binding*. The *wsdlUrl* informs the url where the wsdl can be accessed from; *operation* is the serviceÕs operation name; and *portType* and *binding* determine which portType and binding defined in the wsdl will be used.

The *dataInputBinding* specifies the variable binds required for each type of operation. Each operation input must be a value associated through a *variableBinding*. Thereunto, the *variableBinding* has four attributes: *variableName*, *global*, *type*, and *expression*. *VariableName* indicates the variable's name. The *global* tag is a boolean value used to distinguish global and local variables. If the value is **true**, the global variable denoted in *variableName* will be selected. Otherwise, a local variable is created with type denoted through the attribute type. The attribute expression denotes an XPATH expression. It defines the operationÕs parameter the *variableBinding* refers to. It works for simple or complex types and refers to the SOAP request message of this operation.

The SOAP message includes the current value of the referred global variable. However, when a local variable is used, the user must provide the value for the SOAP message when the referred activity is selected.

The *dataOutputBinding* is very similar to the *dataInputBinding* since it has a list of *variableBinding*. However, *dataOutputBinding* represents a global variable update through the operation response. When an operation is invoked, its return is caught by a *variableBinding* and some global variables are updated. Hence, in an output binding, all the variables are global and, because of this, the tags *global* and *type* are not necessary. Besides that, the expression attribute refers to an XPATH expression that will be used to select a value from the SOAP response message. Then, the referred global variable value will be updated to this value.

This process definition is the user input to the system. The user must also inform the set of business rules to the rule engine. The template of business rules and their definition depends on the type of business rule engine the system will adopt.

4.2 Overview

A declarative web-service orchestrator interacts with the web-services and a rule engine. Figure 1 shows an overview of the interaction or the orchestrator and the rule engine, web services, and users.

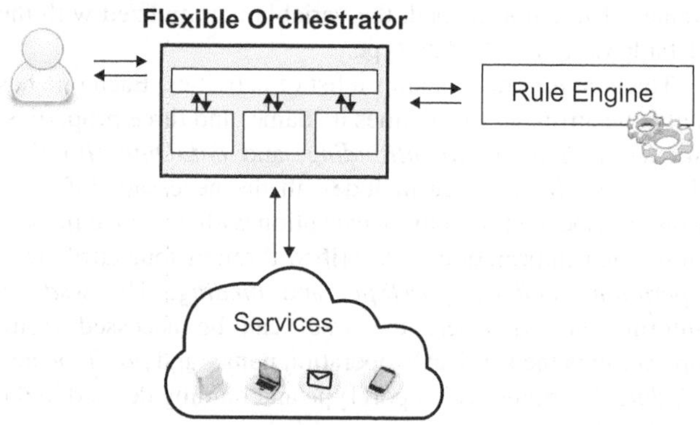

Fig. 1: Overview of the proposed web-service orchestrator.

The main component is the Flexible Orchestrator since it is responsible for interacting with all the others components. Its internal behaviors and architecture are explained in next subsection.

Through an user interface, the user can choose the next activity to be executed by the declarative web-service orchestrator. The user interface shows the enabled activities, the current states of the global data, and if the process termination is enabled or not.

When an activity is selected, the Flexible Orchestrator invokes the correct web service and then waits for the response. It notifies the rule engine whenever an activity is executed. The rule engine is responsible for checking all the business rules and updates the process instance status. Every time the process instance status changes, the Flexible Orchestrator updates the user interface with the set of activities enabled to execute.

An external system can plug its own implementation of the rule engine or adopt a available one. This rule engine must know all the rules and must listen and generate some events expected by our solution. Every time an activity is executed, the Flexible Orchestrator generates the event *DONE(activityName)* and sends it to the rule engine(s). In order to update the process instance status, we expect some events: *ENABLED(activityName)*, *DISABLED(activityName)*, *ENABLED_END()*, and *DISABLED_END()*. Hence, the rule engine must generate these events for the correct interaction with our declarative web service.

4.3 Architecture

Figure 2 presents the architecture of the proposed flexible web-service orchestrator.

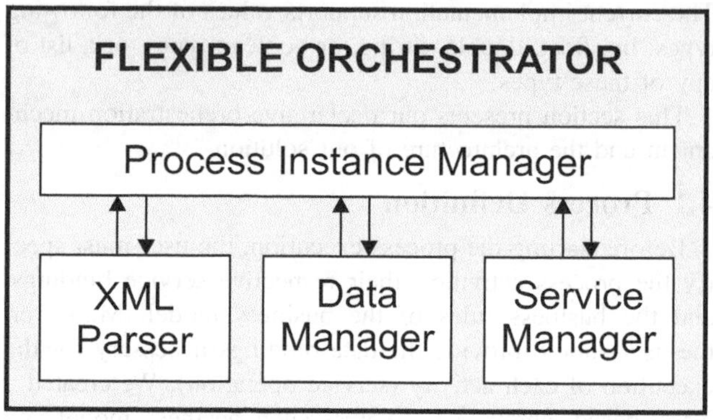

Fig. 2: The architecture of the web-service orchestrator.

Our solution contains four main components:

- **XML Parser:** reads the user input (xml) and parses it in order to make it readable by the Process Instance Manager.
- **Data Manager:** stores the global variables and controls their accesses and updates.
- **Service Manager:** invokes the service operations. This component is responsible for creating the SOAP request message, invoking the service, reading the SOAP response message, and giving the requested results to the Process Instance Manager every time an activity is chosen to be executed.
- **Process Instance Manager:** this is the component that controls the whole flow of a process instance execution. It is responsible for interacting with the other components and the user interface. When the execution starts, it interacts to the XML Parser in order to parse the user input. After receiving the activities and global variables, the execution can actually start. When the user selects an activity to be executed, the Process Instance Manager requests to the Data Manager the necessary data to the variable bindings and then the correct bindings are done. In the sequence, it forwards this information to the Service Manager and waits for its response. When the Service Manager returns the requested data, the output bindings are then made. Besides that, this component interacts with the rule engine in order to update the group of enabled activities.

5. Case Study

In order to demonstrate the use of our declarative web-service orchestrator, this section presents a case study. It consists of an example of declarative process. We demonstrate how to use our declarative orchestrator to control the execution of two different instance of this process.

A business process of a travel agency is used in this section to exemplify the usage of our orchestrator. This is a declarative process expressed using activities and rules. The travel agency can book flight tickets and/or hotels. When the travel agency faces an international transaction, it can convert currencies.

The travel agency contains three services. Each operator of a service is considered as a business process activity. Table 1 details the three services, their operations, and the input and output parameters of each operation.

Table 1: Services details.

FLIGHT SERVICE		
Operations	**Input**	**Output**
checkFlightPrice	- from - to - date - airline	- flightId - price
bookFlight	- flightID	- bookID
payFlightBooking	- bookID - value - creditCard	- paid - paymentCode
HOTEL SERVICE		
Operations	**Input**	**Output**
checkHotel	- hotelName - checkInDate - checkOutDate	- roomsAvailable
bookHotel	- hotelName - checkInDate - checkOutDate - persons	- bookID - bookValue
payHotelBooking	- bookID - value - creditCard	- paid - paymentCode
CURRENCY SERVICE		
Operations	**Input**	**Output**
convertCurrency	- value - fromCurrency - toCurrency	- newCurrency

The declarative business process for the travel agency is a set of business rules, defining constraints to control the set of activities is enabled to execute at each execution point. The process has five rules:

1) It is not possible to book a flight without checking its price before.
2) If a flight is booked, a payment for this booking must be done after that.
3) If the customer wants to book a flight, its price must be checked at least in two different airlines.
4) It is not possible to book a hotel without checking it before.
5) If a hotel is booked, a payment for this booking must be done after that.

One can notice that the currency service was not mentioned among the business rules. This means that the user can choose currency operations at any time while executing the business process, which characterize the flexibility provided by declarative processes.

After modeling the declarative business process, one must link each activity in the process to the corresponding web service. The orchestrator uses this information to perform the service bindings when an activity (service operation) is executed. The code XML 2 presents the variables used in this case study. The code only describes the XML definition for the *payFlightBooking* activity. This activity has references to local variables, whose values are provided by the user during runtime.It also has references to global variables. For example the input parameter *bookValue*, which is the return value of the activity *bookFlight*.

```
<process>
  <globalData>
    <variable name="flightID" type="STRING"/>
    <variable name="prices" type="DOUBLE_LIST"/>
    <variable name="bookID" type="STRING"/>
    <variable name="bookValue" type="DOUBLE"/>
    <variable name="paid" type="BOOLEAN"/>
    <variable name="paymentCode" type="INT"/>
    <variable name="roomsAvailable" type="INT"/>
    <variable name="newCurrency" type="DOUBLE"/>
  </globalData>
  <activities>
    <activity name="payFlightBooking">
      <serviceBinding operation="payFlightBooking"
        wsdlUrl="http://...FlightService?wsdl"
        portType="FlightServicePortType"
        binding="FlightServiceSOAP11Binding"/>
      <dataInputBinding>
        <variableBinding variableName="bookID"
          global="true"
          expression="xpath:/payFB/bookID"/>
        <variableBinding variableName="value"
          global="false" type="DOUBLE"
          expression="xpath:/payFB/value"/>
        <variableBinding variableName="creditCard"
          global="false" type="STRING"
```

```
        expression="xpath:/payFB/creditCard"/>
      </dataInputBinding>
      <dataOutputBinding>
        <variableBinding
        variableName="paid"
        expression="//payFB/result/paid"/>
        <variableBinding
        variableName="paymentCode"
        expression="//payFB/result/pCode"/>
      </dataOutputBinding>
    </activity>
    . . .
  </activities>
</process>
```

XML 2: Process Definition of Case Study

In order to exemplify how the proposed orchestrator works, we will show two different executions of the travel agency business process.

Before starting the process execution, the orchestrator requests the engine the process initial state. The rule engines notifies that the activities *ckeckFlightPrice*, *checkHotel*, and *convertCurrency* are enabled. The other activities *bookFlight*, *payFlightBooking*, *bookHotel*, *convertCurrency* are disabled. The process termination is also enabled at this execution point. This happens because the process does not obligate the execution of any activity before the process termination.

5.1 First execution

Let us assume that a customer wants to buy an international flight ticket. The flight ticket is sold in dollar, but this is not the local currency. Hence, the currency service will be useful for this execution.

The *checkFlightPrice* activity is enabled at the process initial state. The travel agency employee decides to execute this service. He provides the origin and destination places, the flight date, and the airline company as input parameters. The service returns the flight identifier and add its price to the list *prices*. After the service execution, the orchestrator sends a *DONE(checkFlightPrice)* event to the rule engine. According to the rules, the set of activities enabled is not modified after executing the *checkFlightPrice* activity. Thus, the engine does not send any event back.

Afterwards, according to rule 3, the travel agency employee checks the flight price in other airline. When the rule engine receives the *DONE(checkFlightPrice)* event again, it sends the *ENABLED(bookFlight)* event back to the orchestrator, according to rules 1 and 3. One can notice that the *checkFlightPrice* activity continues to be enabled. Thus, if the travel agency employee wants to check flight price in another airline, she can repeat the operation an unlimited number of times.

The travel agency employee, along with the customer, decides to book one of the flights checked. But, before that, the customer wants to know the flight price in the local currency. For that, the employee executes the *convertCurrency* service, which does not modify the activities state. When the client authorizes, the employee books the flight. At this moment, when the rule engine receives the *DONE(bookFlight)* event, it returns *ENABLED(payFlightBooking)* and *DISABLED_END()* events. This last event was received because, according to rule 2, the activity *payFlightBooking* must necessarily be executed before the end of the process.

When the customer decides to pay its flight booking, the employee executes the payFlightBooking service. Only this activity is mandatory at the current execution point. The process termination activity cannot be enabled if this activity is not executed.

5.2 Second execution

Let us now assume that a customer wants to book a hotel in another city of the same country. For this execution, the currency service will not be used.

At the beginning, the travel agency employee check hotels in the desired city. For that, he executes *checkHotel* service informing the hotel name, and check-in and check-out dates. This service returns the number of rooms available in the hotel. After the execution of this service, and according to rule 4, the rule engine generates to the orchestrator the *ENABLED(bookHotel)* event.

The customer decides to book certain hotel, and the travel agency employee makes his booking. This action makes the engine to enable the *payHotelBooking* service. The engine also disables the process termination (through the *DISABLED_END()* event) because the *payHotelBooking* activity is now obliged to be executed before the end of the process, according to rule 5.

In another occasion, but before paying its hotel booking, the customer could decide to check other hotels. Hence, the employee executes the *checkHotel* many times in order to find a hotel that pleasure the customer. Executing the *checkHotel* service many times does not violate any rule. When he finds one, he books this hotel, and then the customer can pay for his booking. From this moment, the process execution for this customer can be finished since there is no mandatory activity pending.

One can perceive that according to the business process defined through business rules, the activities can be executed in any order and/or how many times it is necessary if this execution does not violate any rule.

6. Conclusions

This work proposes a web-service orchestrator for executing declarative business processes. This kind of business process models rely on business rules to describe the behavior of the process and to control the execution of process instances. When working with such a model, the users are driven by the system to produce required results, while the manner in which the results are produced depends on the preferences of users.

Some of the already existent orchestrators provide a static execution, such as the ones that use the BPEL standards. Other orchestrators are more adaptive and allow dynamic composition, but they only provide runtime binding with some pre-modeled compositions. In turn, our proposed orchestrator makes service composition at runtime, binding the output data of a service to the input data of another service.

Our orchestrator receives a declarative process as input. The user also provide the service binding with the process activities, and the data bindings. For this, we defined an XML-based language to specify the business model and services properties.

Our complete solution interacts with a business rule engine. This engine receives and sends events to the orchestrator in order to check the business rules and update the process instance status.

To demonstrate our orchestrator, we showed two different executions of a same business process. The business process presented as example is declarative, and it is expressed by activities and rules. Through the different executions, it is possible to notice the flexibility to choose the order of activities executions and how our orchestrator binds data between services.

Acknowledgment

This work was partly supported by the Brazilian Research Council(CNPq[1]), grants PQ 314539/2009-3, GD 140512/2009-8, GD 142032/2010-7, and CESAR[2].

References

[1] A. Poduval, D. Todd, and H. Gaur, *Do More with SOA Integration: Best of Packt*. Livery Street Birmingham, UK: Packt Publishing, 2011.

[2] H. Kacem, W. Sellami, and A. Kacem, "A formal approach for the validation of web service orchestrations," in *Enabling Technologies: Infrastructure for Collaborative Enterprises (WETICE), 2012 IEEE 21st International Workshop on*, june 2012, pp. 42 –47.

[3] F. Rosenberg and S. Dustdar, "Towards a distributed service-oriented business rules system," in *Proceedings of the Third European Conference on Web Services*, ser. ECOWS '05. Washington, DC, USA: IEEE Computer Society, 2005, pp. 14–. [Online]. Available: http://dx.doi.org/10.1109/ECOWS.2005.28

[4] X. Chen, H. Zeng, and T. Wu, "Decentralized orchestration with local centralized orchestration for composite web services," in *Proceedings of the 2010 International Conference on Parallel and Distributed Computing, Applications and Technologies*, ser. PDCAT '10. Washington, DC, USA: IEEE Computer Society, 2010, pp. 255–260. [Online]. Available: http://dx.doi.org/10.1109/PDCAT.2010.16

[5] S. Nurcan, "A survey on the flexibility requirements related to business processes and modeling artifacts," in *HICSS '08: Proceedings of the 41st Annual Hawaii International Conference on System Sciences*. Washington, DC, USA: IEEE Computer Society, 2008, p. 378.

[1]http://www.cnpq.br

[2]http://www.cesar.org.br

[6] M. Pesic, "Constraint-based workflow management systems: Shifting control to users," Ph.D. dissertation, Technische Universiteit Eindhoven, Eindhoven, The Netherlands, 2008.

[7] W. M. P. van der Aalst and M. Pesic, "Decserflow: Towards a truly declarative service flow language," in *The Role of Business Processes in Service Oriented Architectures, 16.07. - 21.07.2006*, ser. Dagstuhl Seminar Proceedings, F. Leymann, W. Reisig, S. R. Thatte, and W. M. P. van der Aalst, Eds., vol. 06291. Internationales Begegnungs- und Forschungszentrum fuer Informatik (IBFI), Schloss Dagstuhl, Germany, 2006.

[8] M. Pesic and W. M. P. van der Aalst, "A declarative approach for flexible business processes management," in *Business Process Management Workshops*, ser. Lecture Notes in Computer Science, J. Eder and S. Dustdar, Eds., vol. 4103. Springer, 2006, pp. 169–180.

[9] P. Browne, *JBoss Drools Business Rules*. Packt Publishing, 2009.

[10] E. F. Hill, *Jess in Action: Java Rule-Based Systems*. Greenwich, CT, USA: Manning Publications Co., 2003.

[11] S. Bhansali and B. N. Grosof, "Extending the sweetdeal approach for e-procurement using sweetrules and ruleml," in *Proceedings of the First international conference on Rules and Rule Markup Languages for the Semantic Web*, ser. RuleML'05. Berlin, Heidelberg: Springer-Verlag, 2005, pp. 113–129. [Online]. Available: http://dx.doi.org/10.1007/11580072_10

[12] M. Pesic, H. Schonenberg, and W. van der Aalst, "Declare: Full support for loosely-structured processes," in *Enterprise Distributed Object Computing Conference, 2007. EDOC 2007. 11th IEEE International*, oct. 2007, p. 287.

[13] B. Orriens, J. Yang, and M. Papazoglou, "A rule driven approach for developing adaptive service oriented business collaboration," in *In: ICSOC*, 2005, pp. 61–72.

[14] T. Andrews, F. Curbera, H. Dholakia, Y. Goland, J. Klein, F. Leymann, K. Liu, D. Roller, D. Smith, S. Thatte, *et al.*, "Business process execution language for web services," 2003.

[15] H. Weigand, W.-J. van den Heuvel, and M. Hiel, "Business policy compliance in service-oriented systems," *Information Systems*, vol. 36, no. 4, pp. 791 – 807, 2011, <ce:title>Selected Papers from the 2nd International Workshop on Similarity Search and Applications SISAP 2009</ce:title>. [Online]. Available: http://www.sciencedirect.com/science/article/pii/S0306437910001377

[16] A. Strunk, R. Reichert, and E. Schill, "An infrastructure for supporting rebinding in bpel processes," 2009.

[17] G. Canfora, M. Di Penta, R. Esposito, and M. L. Villani, "A framework for qos-aware binding and re-binding of composite web services," *J. Syst. Softw.*, vol. 81, no. 10, pp. 1754–1769, Oct. 2008. [Online]. Available: http://dx.doi.org/10.1016/j.jss.2007.12.792

[18] M. Koning, C.-a. Sun, M. Sinnema, and P. Avgeriou, "Vxbpel: Supporting variability for web services in bpel," *Inf. Softw. Technol.*, vol. 51, no. 2, pp. 258–269, Feb. 2009. [Online]. Available: http://dx.doi.org/10.1016/j.infsof.2007.12.002

[19] A. Charfi and M. Mezini, "Ao4bpel: An aspect-oriented extension to bpel," *World Wide Web*, vol. 10, no. 3, pp. 309–344, Sept. 2007. [Online]. Available: http://dx.doi.org/10.1007/s11280-006-0016-3

[20] G. Hermosillo, L. Seinturier, and L. Duchien, "Using complex event processing for dynamic business process adaptation," in *Services Computing (SCC), 2010 IEEE International Conference on*, july 2010, pp. 466 –473.

[21] Z. Xiao, D. Cao, C. You, and H. Mei, "Towards a constraint-based framework for dynamic business process adaptation," in *Proceedings of the 2011 IEEE International Conference on Services Computing*, ser. SCC '11. Washington, DC, USA: IEEE Computer Society, 2011, pp. 685–692. [Online]. Available: http://dx.doi.org/10.1109/SCC.2011.95

[22] M. Colombo, E. Di Nitto, and M. Mauri, "Scene: a service composition execution environment supporting dynamic changes disciplined through rules," in *Proceedings of the 4th international conference on Service-Oriented Computing*, ser. ICSOC'06. Berlin, Heidelberg: Springer-Verlag, 2006, pp. 191–202. [Online]. Available: http://dx.doi.org/10.1007/11948148_16

Improving Platform Independent Graphical Performance by Compressing Information Transfer using JSON

T.H. McMullen and K.A. Hawick
Computer Science, Massey University, North Shore 102-904, Auckland, New Zealand
email: timmy361@gmail.com, k.a.hawick@massey.ac.nz
Tel: +64 9 414 0800 Fax: +64 9 441 8181

April 2013

ABSTRACT

Interactive animation and other graphical applications are emerging as viable web services in a number of contexts including gaming and simulation. An important part of the performance tradeoff space is balancing the amount of processing work done on (usually slower) rendering clients against that on (usually faster) servers and therefore also the amount of fully or partially processed data that must be transferred across the network connection. This is particularly important when tablet computers and other lower end performance clients are used. Portable or platform independent graphics rendering can be achieved using web clients and we present software architectural ideas and prototypes using JSON and WebGL-based technologies and appropriate data compression and partial processing approaches. We give some performance data and a discussion of the implications for future high-performance platform independent graphics.

KEY WORDS
JavaScript, JSON; graphics performance; platform-independence; compressed information; graphical web-services.

1 Introduction

The problem of implmenting complex graphical rendering applications [5, 9] on new emerging and especially mobile platforms [11, 13] is a challenging one. Whenever a new device is created, with it a new platform for applications to be deployed on tends to emerge. Graphical applications are no exception to this. This paper discusses the current limitations of platform independent graphical application, along with ways to overcome many of them. To achieve this platform independence, and help to improve performance, JSON files are used, along with binary files. As we wish for the applications designed to be platform independent we have based our research on web based technologies, and with it WebGL [1, 2, 4, 6] and JavaScript.

JavaScript is an interpreted programing language, and is heavily used to allow for browser to run client side scripts. JavaScript Object Notation (JSON) is a file format which is able to store data structures. These files can easily parsed and have their associated members, and variables accessed by another program. WebGL is the newest method to achieve platform independent graphics. It is based on OpenGL 2.0 [3, 15] and is implemented using a JavaScript [7, 8] API.

As WebGL uses OpenGL [10, 14] Shading Language (GLSL) to process objects, and create renderings, this allows for many existing shader models to be easily converted to work within this web based environment. One consideration to make when designing an application using WebGL is support, and limitation of hardware on mobile devices. Many smart phones, such as the Samsung Galaxy S3, or Google Nexes 7 are able to run WebGL applications, but due to fewer cores on the GPU, along with a larger limitation on bandwidth this leads to some negative effects. As such applications developed need to take this into consideration, and adapt to suit the run time environment. This can be achieved by various means including reducing the precision of the variables within the shader, or by using fewer uniform variables on the shader.

The JSON file type is based on JavaScripts method for representing data structures, and is human readable. This relationship allows for the information contained within a JSON file to easily be parsed into a JavaScript variable. As these files integrate easily into JavaScript they become an ideal method for passing model files to WebGL for rendering. Converting from standard model files such as wavefont OBJ, and collada to a JSON as well as a converter to binary was necessary, and this has been achieved by using designing a plug in for some 3d modeling applications, along with other programs.

By using JavaScript embedded into HTML5, this allows an application to take advantage of many new features. These new features which can be utilized within a graphical application of this kind, includes the use of Web storage, in which it allows for some data which has previously being downloaded to be accessed without the need to redownload. Another use is that of offline web applications, these allow for an application to be run using previously accessed data, which may be stored in an SQL based database [12] , and cached data.

With all web based applications there is always the challenge of testing performance of a application vs the bandwidth required to transfer data to and from it. This can lead to the challenge of finding the ideal trade off between data transfer, and performance to create an application which is able to be loaded quickly, and runs as fast as it can on its deployed platform. Converting conventional model files into more web technology friendly file types helps to greatly improve both performance and bandwidth.

In this present article we investigate the architectural approach of creating an application using this web based method of implementing platform independent graphics. We create an application which will not become outdated as rapidly and will remain support as long as the devices are compatible with the HTML5 standard.

Our article is structured as follows: In Section 2 we talk about ways in which to setup and utilize WebGL along with different methods in doing so based on various file types. This includes passing data, along with how it is represented and stored within WebGL and JavaScript. Within Section 3 the ways in which optimization have been applied, along with the resulting improvements, in both the start up, and rendering times of the applications. Section 4 discusses the benchmarks, and how they were created, as well as some limitations which were incurred. The final Section 5 is the resulting conclusions of the implementations, and improvements found, along with some future work.

2 Implementation Strategies

This paper works to find ways of optimizing platform independent graphics, using WebGL by using customized file types. We first look into the ways of setting up the scene, and the models to be rendered. secondly the issue of loading in the required data, based on different file types, and finally the rate in which we are able to render objects to screen. A basic overview of these steps follows.

To render an object within WebGL, we need to know two things, firstly the positioning of each point which make up the object, and secondly how each of these points connect. Additional information includes normals and texture concordats, along with anything else needed to help improve the image quality of the produced scene. WebGL uses vertex buffer objects (vbo) to store the information for objects. To setup each of these VBOS the data for each file is read in, and bound to a respective buffer. It is these buffers which gone through and used to draw the object.

Loading in model files for using within WebGL can be done using XMLHttpRequest (XHR) these will load files and processes the data as required. Once a file has been loaded the data from within is parsed to the required vbo. Once the data is passed and the vbo setup correctly WebGL is able to draw an object to screen.

Many existing methods exist for loading models into a WebGL environment one of the more popular by using the JSON file formate, as it is implemented easily within JavaScript. The JSON formate allows for a model to be created and be processed into the required formate for it to be easily converted and passed into a vbo (vertex buffer object). The JSON method is popular as it greatly simplifies the process of loading an object, as it is setup correctly to be used within WebGL. By comparison to use a wavefont OBJ file requires a substantial set up time, as all the information needs to be read, but then also converted into new arrays. This conversion process uses the face values in the OBJ file represented by a line in the file starting with "f", then using the values on which follow to determine how to make up that face. By using a JSON file this process is done offline and will not unnecessarily impede performance at start up. By comparing these two file types, it is clear to see that the JSON file will be faster to start up, but both are set up in the same way with each piece of information taking up its own buffer.

Once again we are able to improve upon this method by using VBOS and there ablility to have offsets assigned within them, this allows for a single vbo to contain multiple types of data, for example having one array containing all positioning data, texture coordinates and normals, while another stores the indices. By using these offsets within a vbo it removes the need to switch between buffers multiple times for each draw call. This can easily be achieved by using a binary file in place or alongside a JSON file. Algorithm 1 below shows the basis of the proccess in which is followed when wanting to reader a scene from this file type and method. Firstly the position attributes within the vertex shader are enabled, so it can be passed data, this is done for all attributes of the shader which will be passed data. The next step is to bind our position buffer, this is what is read in from the JSON file, and contains the positioning data for each point of the model. This information is then passed the the appropriate attribute on the shader to be processed when needed. This step needs to be repeated for each variable which you are using, in this case the texture data, along with the normals data. Finally the indices are bound and used to draw the elements above.

Algorithm 1 Basic steps used in the process of drawing a frame. Requires a lot of addition work which could be simplified by using fewer arrays.

---

declare $position[]$, $texture[]$, $normals[]$, $indices[]$
enable position, within the shader program
enable texture, within the shader program
enable normals, within the shader program
bind position
link position array to the shader
bind texture
link texture array to the shader
bind normals
link normals array to the shader
bind indices
draw elements within the above arrays, based on indices

By switching to use a binary file to store the required information, the file size will decrease, improving on the start up time, and no longer needing to conver a string to floats also will improve this time. To use this method a model is exported into a binary file, where the first few bits tell you how each of the arrays stored are, along with what each part means, and where the offsets are, and how large they are. Once the file is loaded it is then split up and two new buffers are created from the array. Using JavaScript we are able to take this header information, and create new arrays based on the data from another and taking very specific parts. For this instance the requirements were one 32float array for storing the more complex information, and another 16 unsigned integer array for storing the indices. By using the offset within the buffers, the program will skip a set amount of bits within the array, and will know how and where to access the relevant information for rendering an object within WebGL.

Algorithm 2 Similar to Algorithm 1, but by using fewer buffers, increase the speed at which each frame can be processed.

---

declare $faceBuffer[]$, $indices[]$
enable position, within the shader program
enable texture, within the shader program
enable normals, within the shader program
bind faceBuffer
link positions based on data from the faceBuffer
link texture based on data from the faceBuffer
link normals based on data from the faceBuffer
bind indices
draw elements within the above arrays, based on indices

Algorithm 2 above shows a similar process as in Algorithm 1, but with fewer steps. In this implementation, the attributes still are required to be enabled, but only the one buffer, in this case faceBuffer is used, because of this when the data is linked to the attribute on the shader it uses an offset to skip a set amount of information each time. By having this offset this allows for the one buffer to hold all the information on the object or model removing the need to switch between buffers and bind multiple buffers each call. The final step remains the same as it is in algorithm 1.

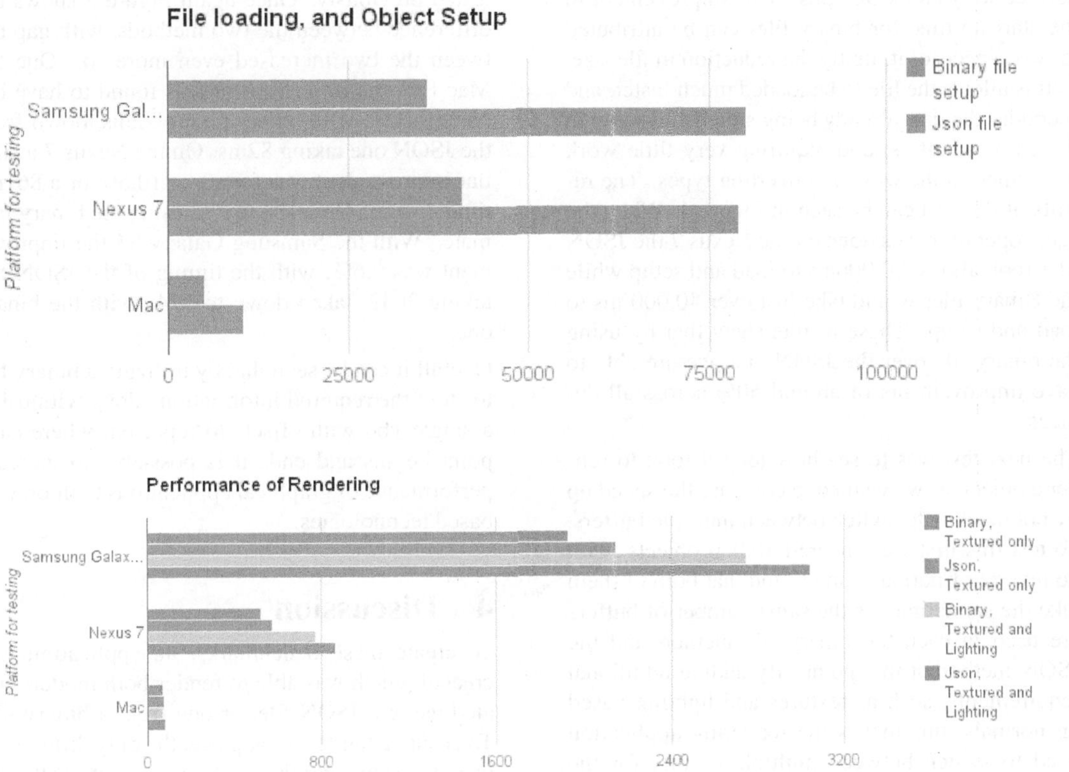

Figure 1: Time to load in and Setup 1,000 instances of the Utah Teapot (ms) - above; and time to render 10,000 frames – below

3 Selected Results

Figure 1 shows the times for various devices to load in and setup 1,000 instances of the standard Utah teapot model (above) and the times to render 10,000 frames containing it (below).

To test the performance increase by switching file types several aspects of the rendering application were timed. Firstly time taken to load in files and set up the arrays and as such the corresponding VBOS. The next tests consisted of testing the time taken to render an object in different conditions, such as with or with out textures or lighting, as each of these will alter the performance of the applications and GPU. The devices which were used for testing were a Mac Pro with two AMD 5770 GPUs, 8 Gbs Ram, and a quad core 3.2 Ghz processor, an Google Nexus 7, and a Samsung Galaxy S3. These devices were chosen as the performance difference between them and architecture can demonstrate how that will effect the testing environment, and as such an application which is implemented with this kind of technology

The first test took a wavefont OBJ file containing texture information along with normals, this was then converted into two different files, firstly a JSON file, with each array setup, then into a binary file. This resulted in turning a 94.8 kb OBJ file into a 36.9 kb binary file, significantly reducing the bandwidth required to transfer the file. This reduction in size, and improvement in format also helped in the time taken to setup a file. In testing the time taken to load 1000 instances of the same model, and set up the correct arrays, it took 19489ms to load and convert the OBJ files, by comparison the JSON files took 10415ms which is a good improvement. The binary file though was far superior to these two other approaches, in which the time taken to load in 1000 files, and set up the correct arrays took 5092ms. This improvement in the start up time for binary files can be attributed to two aspects of it, firstly the reduction in file size, as this allows the file to be loaded much faster, and secondly the data already being stored and setup in the correct buffers, and requiring very little work performed in the way of converting types. The results of this test can be seen in Figure 4. When the same operation was done on the Nexus 7 the JSON files took almost 80,000ms to load and setup while the Binary files would take just over 40,000 ms to load and setup. These results show that by using the binary file over the JSON one, we are able to have improvements of around 50% across all devices.

The next test was to see how long it took to render a object, as we wanted to compare the speed up by not needing to switch between multiple buffers. To test this first we rendered 10,000 objects, with no texture or normals, and found that both of them take the same time, as the same number of buffers are used in each the binary file method and the JSON method at this point. By adding additional requirements, such as textures and lighting based on normals, this makes the rendering application need to switch between multiple buffers for the JSON file, but not for a binary one. With this test we found that once again that the binary file, and using an offset within a vbo proved to be a more effective method of processing. Figure 5 clearly shows that these results are true across all devices tested on. When tested on the Mac Pro the improvement was found to be 9.3%, as the JSON implementation took 75ms to complete while the binary one took a total of 68ms. The Nexus 7 the improvement was found to be 8.7%, with a time of 571 from the JSON file, to 519ms with the binary one. Finally the Samsung Galaxy S3 showed an improvement of 8.0%, with the binary file taking only 1928ms compared to the JSON one of 2096 ms.

For the last test, we compared the performance of the JSON and binary implementation again, but with also using normals, as to apply a lighting effect to the model, as seen in figure 3. This resulted as expected with an increase in time taken the reader the scene, caused by the increased requirements of the shader, along with the increase in data required to be passed. The improvement in performance of the binary implementation also increased over the JSON method, more than was tested previously. Once again Figure 5 shows the difference between the two methods, with gap between the two increased even more so. One the Mac Pro, the improvement was found to have become 12.2% with binary taking 72ms, down from the JSON one taking 82ms. On the Nexus 7 a similar improvement was found, at 10.5% or a 861ms time using JSON files, to 772 using the binary format. With the Samsung Galaxy S3 the improvement was 9.6%, with the timing of the JSON file taking 3042, taken down to 2748 with the binary one.

Overall it can be seen that by utilizing a binary file to store the required information, along with using a single vbo with offsets to represent where each point begins and ends it is possiable to increase performance of graphical applications built on web based technologies.

4 Discussion

To create these benchmarks, an application was created which was able to render both models created using a JSON file, or one from a binary file. To ensure a fair test took place, the only differences were the setup and the rendering aspects of the application. Each of the two areas were tested separately as to ensure that the start up time did not affect the rendering timing.

The images below show the different effects applied to the teapot throughout the different stages of testing. Below in image Figure 2,is the effect of rendering the Utah teapot without any additional information. This implementation was the most simplistic as it used the least amount of information, and thus the least amount of processing by the graphics card. The implementation did not effect the performance, as the data which was passed, and how it was processed was the same for both binary and JSON files.

Figure 3 shows the uses of textures applied to the Utah teapot. In this implementation we see the first performance increase of the binary file and using offest within buffers. As shown in Figure 5 across all platforms tested, the binary was faster in rendering each frame than the JSON implementation, as it no longer is required to switch between buffers so rapidly. One thing to note is that the longer the renderings take to complete, the smaller the improvement was found to be.

Figure 2: Utah Teapot, being rendered with not applied textured or lighting

Figure 3: Utah Teapot, being rendered with an applied texture

Once the testing started to include the use of more information, it became clear that the binary file became far more effect because of the way in which it renders an object. In Figure 4 we see the application of the lightning based on the normals passed through to the shader. By using the binary and offset data we are able to minimize the need to switch between 3 buffers to the use of only one, this improvement would become more prevalent with the more information being passed at a time.

One area looked into to help improve testing was designing a Chrome plug-in to help in capturing detailed performance, this proved to be unnecessary, as the best way to measure performance was found to be using the console within Chrome, with could also be accessed easily on android based devices.

With testing it was found that based on the firmware running on the device would affect its implementation. With the Samsung Galaxy S3, some fireware would not allow for the use of high precision data types on the shader, meaning that to test on this device a medium precision would need to be used, and this would effect the rendering speed across all devices. This problem was found to only occur on some firmware so did not effect the testing when run on firmware.

Figure 4: Utah Teapot, being rendered with an applied texture and lighting

5 Conclusion

In summary we have managed to show two method in which to improve performance of platform independent graphics using WebGL. By converting the file to binary, with the correct arrays setup within, we manage to have a file which loads faster and is ready to be rendered in almost half the time as a JSON file, and one quarter the time of an wavefont OBJ file. The other improvement measured was that of the rendering speed, by removing the need to switch buffers multiple times for each draw call, this lead to the overall improvement of around 10% depending on the device, and amount of information being passed.

We believe that these changes are easily implemented into most applications based on WebGL, and can lead to greatly improved performance of an application, in startup and run time.

Future work would be to convert a JSON file using multiple VBOS, into one which used a single VBO, to allow for the ease of loading in a JSON file, with the performance found with the binary method.

In summary, various mobile devices hold great promise as platforms for rendering complex quality graphical models even using platform independent software and client approaches. Appropriate use of data compression and JSON significantly improves teh performance however.

References

[1] Andersson, S., Goransson, J.: Virtual Texturing with WebGL. Master's thesis, Chalmers University of Technology, Gothenburg, Sweden (2012)

[2] Anttonen, M., Salminen, A.: Building 3d webgl applications. Tech. Rep. Report 16, Tamperer University of Technology, Finland, Department of Software Systems (2011)

[3] Bourke, P.: 3d stereo rendering using opengl (and glut) (2002), website PDF

[4] Chen, B., Xu, Z.: A framework for browser-based multiplayer online games using webgl and websocket. In: Proc. Int. Conf. on Multimedia Technology (ICMT). pp. 471–474. Hangzhou, China (26-28 July 2011)

[5] Congote, J., Segura, A., Kabongo, L., Moreno, A., Posada, J., Ruiz, O.: Interactive visualization of volumetric data with webgl in real-time. In: Proc. 16th Int. Conf. on 3D Web Technology (Web3D'11). pp. 137–145. Paris, France (20-22 June 2011)

[6] DeLillo, B.P.: Webglu development library for webgl. In: Proc. SIGGRAPH 2010. p. 1. Los Angeles, California, USA (25-29 July 2010)

[7] ecma international, Rue du Rhone 114, CH-1204 Geneva: ECMAScript Language Specification, 5.1 edn. (June 2011), standard ECMA-262

[8] amd Fritz Schneider, T.A.P.: JavaScript: the complete reference. McGraw-Hill (2012), iSBN 9780071741200

[9] Hearn, D., Baker, M.P.: Computer Graphics with OpenGL. No. ISBN 0-13-015390-7, Pearson Prentice Hall, third edition edn. (2004)

[10] Hill, F.S.: Computer Graphics Using OpenGL. No. ISBN 0-02-354856-8, Prentice Hall (2001)

[11] McMullen, T.H., Hawick, K.A., Preez, V.D., Pearce, B.: Graphics on web platforms for complex systems modelling and simulation. In: Proc. International Conference on Computer Graphics and Virtual Reality (CGVR'12). pp. 83–89. WorldComp, Las Vegas, USA (16-19 July 2012), cSTN-157

[12] Nixon, R.: PHP, MySQL & JavaScript. No. ISBN 978-0-596-15713-5, O'Reilly (2009)

[13] Preez, V.D., Pearce, B., Hawick, K.A., McMullen, T.H.: Human-computer interaction on touch screen tablets for highly interactive computational simulations. In: Proc. International Conference on Human-Computer Interaction. pp. 258–265. IASTED, Baltimore, USA. (14-16 May 2012)

[14] Woo, M., Neider, J., Davis, T., Shreiner, D.: OpenGL Programming Guide: The Official Guide to Learning OpenGL. Addison-Wesley, 3rd edition edn. (1999), iSBN:0201604582

[15] Wright, R.S., Haemel, N., Sellers, G., Lipchak, B.: OpenGL Superbible. No. ISBN 978-0-321-71261-5, Pearson, fifth edn. (2011)

EV-IMP Model: A comprehensive model for evaluation of an organization's website success

A. Sherafat[1]**, A. Pouriyeh**[2]**, and M. Doroodchi**[3]
[1] University Of Tehran, Tehran, Iran
[2]North Dakota State University, Fargo, ND, USA
[3]Cardinal Stritch University, Milwaukee, WI, USA

Abstract - *Continuous web site evaluation based on the site alignment with the mission of organization and providing more efficient site is discussed in this paper. This method integrates the quantitative and qualitative evaluation methods to measure the site's success. The indicators are generated and changed throughout time with expert's input.*

Index Terms—**Web site success, success evaluation, performance enhancement.**

I. INTRODUCTION

With the emergence of the internet as a basic infrastructure of the new business model collectively called e-business, almost all companies and organizations tried to have at least a tiny share in this new business environment through their own web sites. In fact, it is now a fact that web sites can help businesses, organizations and companies decrease their cost, provide better interactions with customers, provide smoother and faster processing of customer demands, and provide a more competitive performance. For this reason, organizations are always after determining the effectiveness and success of their websites. Many attempts have been made to define a model-based assessment for web site success. Almost all proposed assessment methods propose a comprehensive model of web site success based on technical issues, web site appearance and usability from user point of view. In this work, besides the mentioned factors we propose a method to evaluate and measure the performance of a particular web site through a framework which includes the following features.

- The site's performance indicators are measured in alignment with the organization's main goals.
- The site's performance continuously is evaluated.
- The evaluation feedback is used to modify the site features.
- The overall performance has to increase with several iterations of the above steps.

The rest of this paper is organized as follows. Next section the overviews the basic concepts of web site evaluation by reviewing the related works. Section 3 covers the proposed model which includes site success evaluation method, identification and correction of the weaknesses to enhance the overall performance. One of the distinguishing characteristics of this model is the integration of quantitative metrics to ordinary qualitative performance indicators in the process of web site evaluation and providing continuous improvement.

II. RELATED WORK

A great deal of effort has been done to define comprehensive and effective factors to measure the success of websites. Some approaches put more weight on technical issues while others try to show that business performance features such as service quality and customer satisfaction play more important roles in web site success. One of the recent approaches is known as 2QCV3Q model which is for evaluation of website quality based on both owner and user viewpoints [1]. The 2QCV3Q method is a 'multi-stakeholder' approach in which the viewpoints of all involved stakeholders are considered simultaneously including the site's main stakeholders including the owner, users, and those involved in the design and implementation of the site. Site identity, content, service location, management, usability and feasibility are the fundamental dimensions which are used to evaluate a web site through the interview, questionnaire, workgroup sessions and web site visit in this model.

Stockdale, et. al., emphasizes that the quality must precede any measurement of use. Then, the quality-based approach is realized by identifying the three dimensions of quality as system, information and service. In this approach, system quality refers to the elements of a system that have been affected by the end user [2]. For information quality attribute, the content is considered to be the most important element of web site which is directly related to web site success. Service quality in this model shows the importance of service provider within an organization.

A fuzzy model is proposed by Albuquerque and Belchoir considering usability, conceptual reliability and representation reliability through five separated stages [3].

In another work by Fitzpatrick and Higgins [8],a methodical analysis and synthesis of three strands including quality, organizational requirements, and human-computer interaction is discussed.

Each of the mentioned models highlight different aspects of web site success criteria while in this paper we collectively cover all of the aspects of web site success through the proposed model.

III. PROPOSED MODEL

Although there are different approaches to evaluate organization's success based on the functionality of their web sites, almost all of these methods are basically similar to each other from cardinal point of views.

In our proposed model, the concept of Quality Management is used for evaluating organization's success through the functionality of its web site. This technique which is based on European Foundation for Quality Management (EFQM) model covers two critical topics, evaluation and implementation, to define the basic structure regarding evaluation of an organization's web site success.

Figure 1 depicts the four basic concept of proposed model which we call it Evaluation-Improvement method or for short EV-IMP. These components include Objectives, Processes, Indicators/criteria and Feedback that will be explained in the following sections. We reiterate it again here that the main purpose of introducing EV-IMP is to evaluate the organization's success through the appropriate functionality of its web site.

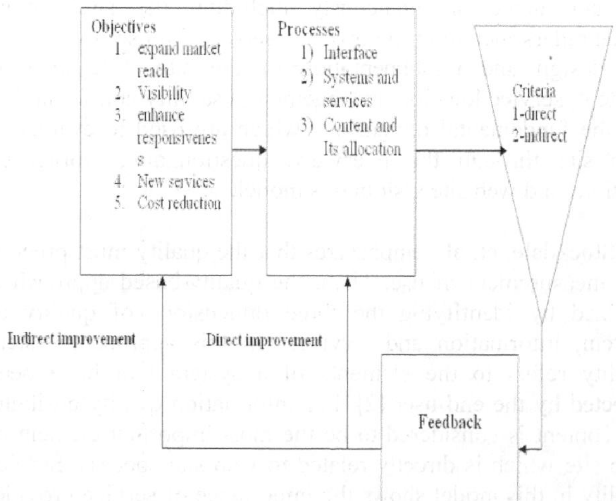

Figure 1: EV-IMP model overview.

The main components of this model are explained in the following.

A) Processes: the main part of EV-IMP model is processes which includes interface, systems and services, content and its allocation[2], [4-5].

1. Interface

This component is related to the website's appearance and interaction with the users and are evaluated by the following factors.

- Visual design principles
- Graphics and multimedia
- Text and style
- Flexibility and adaptability

2. Systems and services

The website's interaction with the target users (for example technical support and services that are given to the customers)are evaluated by the followings factors.

- Accessibility: Is the website easily accessible?
- Usability: Is the website easy to use?
- Functionality: Does the website provide a clear mechanism to achieve the objectives?
- Intractability: Does the website respond well to the user demands?
- Reliability: Is the website reliable?
- Flexibility: Is the website flexible to support different customers and their different demands?
- Security: Is the system safe and secure for sensitive information such as financial interactions and trading?
- Communication: Is it easy and straightforward for site visitors to make contacts with the organization through the site?
- Perception of service: Does the website provide services that the organization cares about them?
- Trust building: Does the website emphasize on building trust with the users?
- Empathy: Does the website create a sense of empathy and the users are recognized by the organization?
- After market service: Do users get after-market services such as tracking, support, etc.?
- Customization: Does the website meet the customer's requirements and intentions?

3. Content and its presentation:

The website's content and the content presentation are evaluated by using the following related aspects.

- Relevance
- Accuracy(authenticity)of the website's content
- Understandable content: Is information is easy to understand?
- Completeness: Does the content covers all the required information?
- Current: Is website's content updated regularly?

- Dynamic content: Does web site's content present diversity and adaptability with regards to the users requirements?
- Personalized: Does website provide personalized services?

B) Objectives: In general, objectives can ultimately expand market reach, increase visibility, enhance responsiveness and reduce cost.

C) Results: They can be in the form of quantitative or qualitative indicators. Qualitative indicators are those indicators which are the result of stakeholders' inference about the quality of the website. On the other hand, Quantitative indicators are gained from statistical data, organizational information and the organization's website service providers. Another primary category that is referred in this model includes direct and indirect indicators. Direct indicators have direct effects on the website's activities and processes while indirect indicators play an important role in organization web site's success through the related organization to review and modify the website's established and developing objectives based on the macro strategies and indirect results.

D) Feedback: it includes the tools for improvement through measuring the results and evaluating them. There are two tools in this model for the evaluation:

- Stakeholders' questionnaire: This tool is designed to evaluate the website from stakeholder's point of view. Each stakeholder's representative must evaluate the website's success from its own point of view and determine the examples and observations which will be possible from the questionnaire analysis.

- Quantitative information: Website statistics and information are gained from the organization and web service providers through the questionnaire which contains quantitative indicators. As mentioned before, this information might have direct effects on the website quality or have indirect effects on the objectives. It is obvious that some of the indicators that are included in the tools have double applications and they can have effects on both the website's processes and the objective.

IV. Evaluation Criteria

Qualitative and quantitative parameters are two basic parts of criteria in this model that will be explained more.

Basically qualitative criteria[1-5] and [8-24] can cover following aspects:

- User friendliness
- Navigability
- Maintenance
- Technology suitability
- Reusability
- Involvement capacity
- Functionality
- Security and integrity
- Content

On the other hand, quantitative criteria [25-30] are included the following topics:

- Basics
- Marketing and profitability
- Support & services

V. Models Details

The website's objectives and the indicators being evaluated by the model's tools play an important role in relationship between three main processes of the web site. These tools include two questionnaires:

1. Qualitative questionnaire inquiring stakeholders about the website's quality in the form of five choices of excellent, good, average, bad, very bad with the score of 100, 75, 50, 25 and 0 respectively, which is designed in the questionnaire. It is related not only to the stake holder's rating but also to the reason they choose that choice.

2. Quantitative questionnaire gathers statistics and required information about the website functionality and its output. These data is achieved through the questionnaire which is given to the organization to gather and represent information from its related sectors or its service providers. In this step processes, objectives, reasons, and indicators scope are rated from 0 to 100.

Through analyzing the result of Qualitative and Quantitative questionnaire, the weak points are extracted and the proper actions are defined. Analyzing will determine that how the website works in different processes of interface, services and systems, and content and its allocation. In the next step, the corrective actions for the successful function of the organization are prioritized and implemented. These evaluation activities can be repeated periodically to have more effects on the organization website's success.

Table 1 shows the relationship between the indicators and the three main processes in the website which is evaluated by this model. The last row of the table contains the percentage of processes scores in the evaluation. For example in the website which has been studied here the interface process has the first rank of weakness with 31%score.

Table1: Scores separated by the triple dimensions of content, service and system, interface. (Case study: a regional electric company's website(YREC))

Indicator	Content	Service/system	Interface
User friendliness	43.75	38.33	50
Navigability	43.75	23.68	25
maintenance	---	68.75	---
Technology suitability	---	66.66	50
Reusability	---	75	---
Involvement capacity	---	12.5	25
Functionality	---	25	25
Security and integrity	37.5	55.55	50
Content	58.33	---	25
Total	50	41.9	31

VI. Model Characteristics

The EV-IMP model has some characteristics that make it different in comparison with other models for evaluation of an organization's success. Some of these specifications are listed as follow:

- Quality management: the model is designed based on the stake holder's needs and the organization's objectives for the website development.
- The indicator's comprehensiveness and completeness: in this model beside the qualitative criteria, the metrics criteria is also considered which is the unique property of this technique.
- Usability: the simple structure of this model makes it possible for variety of users.
- General use: the designed model is usable for a wide range of websites (organizational, personal, educational and e-commerce websites).
- Improvement Consideration: the main objective of this model is website's improvement and promotion based on the organization's objectives.
- Simultaneous attention to effectiveness and efficiency: it can be done by focusing on both technical and organizational aspects of a web site.
- Considering metrics and involving them in the process of the website's evaluation.

VII. Case Study

Yzd regional electric company (YREC) was established in 1986 and has been working in the field of electric power generation, processing, transmission and distribution of Yzd province. To achieve its mission, Yzd regional electric company is composed of five major departments including deputies for operation, design and development, financial, planning and research and human resources.

The YREC website (www.yrec.co.ir) was designed consisting of several main parts in which part there are some menus and internal pages.

Main Menu:

- Sub-sites
- News
- Researches and standards
- Statistic and information
- Tenders and employment
- The subscriber's guidance

It also includes survey part, site features (downloads, video albums...), site statistics, contact us, search facilities and etc. Based on EV-IMP model and after evaluation and assessing website scores, the development project plan for improving the website performance were identified and prioritized. The defined project was implemented within one year and the website was re-evaluated again after that. In the project definition the priority was given to the criteria which gained low scores in spite of their importance. The results of evaluation performed on the qualitative criteria are shown in table 2.

Table2: The qualitative scores of the YREC divided by main criteria

criteria	Before Improvement (%)	After Improvement (%)
User friendliness	45	47
Navigability	21.5	50
Maintenance	68.8	70
Technology Suitability	62.5	60
Reusability	75	70
Involvement Capacity	18.8	35
Functionality	25	37
Security and Integrity	62.5	60
Content	58.3	62

In order to validate the performance of the proposed model, the results were compared against EFQM and close agreements were observe; after the questionnaire was modified and customized, the quantitative criteria questionnaire was given to the planning and research deputy and IT department of Yzd regional electric company so that the related indicators were completed. Then with result evaluation mechanism according to EFQM model, scores were allocated to indicators and sub-indicators.

The qualitative indicators were also identified and improvement projects were defined and implemented and after one year the web site was re-evaluated. Table 3 depicts the results of this part.

Table 3: The quantitative scores of the YREC divided by main criteria

Criteria	Before Improvement (%)	After Improvement (%)
Basics	8	35
Marketing and profitability	2	15
Support & services	3	30

VIII. Conclusion

The method of continuous improvement is realized for website success evaluation through multiple stages based on the alignment of the site with the organizational goals. This obviously includes many efforts to find the deficiencies and adjust them at the proper level. This iterative method continuously gets the feedback and uses them to improve the web site in a systematic model. The test results of aan actual organization website indicates significant efficiency and improvements.

IX. References

[1] Mich, L., Franch, M. &Cilione G. (2003). The 2QCV3Q quality model for the analysis of web site requirements. *Journal of Web Engineering*, 2(1&2), 105-127.

[2] Stockdale, R. and Borovicka, M. &Innsbrck, A. (2006). Using Quality Dimensions in the Evaluation of Websites. *The International Conference2006 ,Citeseer.*

[3] Albuquerque, A.B. &Belchoir, A.D., (2002). E-Commerce Websites: a Qualitative Evaluation. *The 11th International World Wide Web Conference. Hawaii, USA.*

[4] Van der Merwe, R. &Bekker, F. (2003).A framework and methodology for evaluating e-commerce websites. *Retrieved from http://www.emeraldinsight.com*

[5] Guo, S. Shao, B. (2005). Quantitative Evaluation of E-Commercial Websites of Foreign Trade Enterprises. *Retrieved from http://www.doi.ieeecomputersociety.org.*

[6] McCall, J., Richards, P. & Walters, G (1977) Factors in software quality, *Rome Aid Defence Centre, Italy.*

[7] Boëhm, B. (1978). Characteristics of software quality, Vol. 1 of TRW series on software technology, *North-Holland, Amsterdam, Netherlands.*

[8] Fitzpatrick, R. & Higgins, C. (1998). Usable software and its attributes: A synthesis of software quality, European Community law and human-computer interaction, *HCI'98 Conference, Springer, London, UK.*

[9] Fitzpatrick, R. (2002).Additional Quality Factors for the World Wide Web. *Retrieved from http//www.comp.dit.ie/rfitzpatrick/papers/2RF_AQF_WWW.pdf*

[10] Mich, L. &Franch, M. (2002). Requirements for a Tool to Support Evaluation of Web Site Quality based on the 2QCV3Q Model. *Retrieved from http://www.rintonpress.com/xjwe1/jwe-2-1&2/105-127.pdf.*

[11] Mich, L. &Franch, M., (2000). 2QCV2Q: A model for Web sites Analysis and Evaluation. *IRMA '00, Idea Group Publishing, 2000*, 586-589.

[12] Mich, L. Franch, M. Cilione, G. &Marzani, P. (2003).Tourist Destinations and the Quality of Web sites: A Study of Regional Tourist Boards in the Alps. *Retrieved from http://www.ifitt.org*

[13] Mich, L., Franch, M, Novi Inverardi, P.L. & Marzani, P. (2003) Choosing the right weight model for Web site quality evaluation. *The 3rd Int. Conf. on Web Engineering July 14 -18, 2003* , 334-337.

[14] Kececi, N. Abran, A. (2006).Analyzing, assessing & measuring software quality within a logic-basedgraphical *.Retrieved from http://www.gelog.etsmtl.ca.*

[15] Bevan N. (1998).Usability Issues in Web Site Design. *Retrieved from http://www.usabilitynet.org/papers/usweb98.*

[16] Dreyfus, P. (1998).Usability and the Future of the Web. *Retrieved from http://developer.netscape.com/news/viewsource/archive/editor98_1_20.html.*

[17] Keeker, K. (1997).Improving Web Site Usability. *Retrieved from http://msdn.microsoft.com/workshop/management/planning/improvingsiteusa.asp.*

[18] Trower, T. (1999).The Human Factor: Guidelines *.Retrieved from http://www.microsoft.com/devnews/SepOct96/HumanFactor5_5.htm.*

[19] Nielsen, J. (1999) User interface directions for the Web *Communications of the ACM*, 42(1), 65-72.

[20] Gehrke, D &Turban, E. (1999). Determinants of successful Website design: relative importance and recommendations foreffectiveness.*The32nd Annual Hawaii International Conference on System Sciences.*

[21] Ivory, M. Y. et al, (2001). Empirically Validated Web Page Design Metrics. *SIGCHI conference on Human Factors in Computing Systems, March 31-April 4, Seattle, WA, USA.*

[22] Shedroff, N. (2005). Recipe for a successful web site. *Retrieved from http://www.nathan.com*

[23] Dragulanescu, N. (2002).Website Quality Evaluations: Criteria and Tools. *Retrieved from http://www.springerlink.com/index/gj428l8v60874134*

[24] Grannas, J. (2007). What factors are important in developing a successful e-commerce website?.*Retrieved from http://www.hig.diva-portal.org*

[25] Einsburg, B. Novo, J. Shreeve, J. (2001).Introduction to the Guide to Web Analytics *.Retrieved from http://www.futurenow.com.*

[26] Cusack, BO. (2001).Measurements on the Web: Where do they Lead?.*Retrieved from http://www.naccq.ac.nz*

[27] Creese, G and Burby, J. (2005).Web Analytics Key Metrics and KPIs. *Retrieved from http://www.kaushik.net/avinash/waa-kpi-definitions-1-0.pdf*

[28] Stowers, GNL (2004). Measuring the Performance of E-government" *Retrieved from http://www.businessofgovernment.org*

[29] Hatry, p. (2003). Reporting Performance Information: Suggested, Criteria for Effective Communication. *Board of the Financial Accounting Foundation.*

[30] Hatry, Harry P. (1999). Performance Measurement: Getting Results. *Washington, D.C. Urban Institute Press*

SESSION

SEMANTIC WEB

Chair(s)

TBA

A semantic dependency-graph-based approach combining platforms hosting data and applications

Enhancing creative synergistic publishing and organizing scientific competitions on the web

Sayoko Shimoyama, Robert Sidney Cox III, David Gifford and Tetsuro Toyoda
Integrated Database Unit, Advanced Center of Computing and Communication (ACCC), RIKEN
2-1 Hirosawa, Wako, Saitama, 351-0198, Japan.
toyoda.tetsuro@gmail.com

Linked open data increases availability of original scientific and other data. Modifiable or 'forkable' open-source programs hosted on shared platforms make applications utilizing these data ready for reuse. However, data resources and applications are often hidden from each other and external reuse by separation of publication and access to data repositories. We constructed the LinkData.org platform to automate publishing together of linked open data, applications, and introduce the 'dependency graph' illustrating relationships between data, applications and users. Dependency graphs allow transparent evaluation of data and application integration. Data and dependency graphs are accessible with open semantic APIs. Because dependency graphs combine both data and applications published on the platform, users easily create new applications for data and publish new data resources for use with applications. This yields a creative synergy cycle between data publication and application development, as shown applied to a scientific competition for design of synthetic regulatory DNA.

Keywords—semantic web; linked open data; synthetic biology; bioinformatics; data and application web publishing

I. INTRODUCTION

Data repositories and directories for open data such as The Comprehensive Knowledge Archive Network (CKAN) web-based system for the storage and distribution of data, supported by the Open Knowledge Foundation, help users register their data resources and locate related data. Resource Description Framework (RDF) graph structure data format is the standard for sharing linked open data (LOD) on the web.

The LOD model with RDF and SPARQL endpoints gives open access to the data for any external applications (Apps) worldwide, however, the act of separating the data from the applications on the web makes the synergic collaboration between data and applications invisible; resulting in the situation that contributions to opening and maintaining the data are not as appropriately evaluated as the contributions to the Apps, and thus the situation does not motivate academicians to make such contributions as to donate their own datasets.

To overcome this situation, we developed LinkData.org (http://linkdata.org) as a data publishing platform and LinkDataApp (http://app.linkdata.org) as an application publishing platform, and combined them by automatically recording dependency graphs that relate data and Apps using the data; thus, making LinkData as a repository of dependency graphs connecting Apps and datasets, as well as a repository of applications and datasets.

Here we show the cycle actually enhancing various synergistic collaborations and organizing a web-based scientific competition for synthetic biology promoter design. Further LinkData.org displays a usability analysis score calculated based on the dependency graphs to rank highly useful data and applications, so that the scores motivate users to release and update their data and applications, and to trust other's open data.

II. LINKDATA FUNCTIONS

A. LinkData as an RDF publishing platform

1) Support functions for creating table data to upload: As a support function that allows Users to easily define schema, LinkData provides a GUI by which anyone can create and download a template. When a User selects the "Input Table Data" menu and enters metadata for their data using this GUI, a table format Excel file using column names for RDF properties is generated, and this file can be downloaded. Users input their data to the template to create their own table data for uploading.

2) Conversion to RDF format and publishing: Template data tables can be uploaded, converted to RDF format, and published online at LinkData.org. When a User selects "Convert to RDF" and uploads the table data file in Excel or TSV format, anyone accessing the published data's webpage will be able to browse and download the table data, a template for table data, as well as in RDF format.

3) Reuse Data Function: Schemas of all of published Data can be reused for publishing new datasets. Users can activate the reuse table data function at the published Data webpage and download a revisable template to use with their own data.

[Paper Submission for SWWS'13 Conference]

TABLE I. ENTITIES AND LINKS OF LINKDATA CONCEPTS

Entity	Definition	
Data	A single data set which has been published by a User in LinkData	
Application (App)	A single application which has been published by a User in LinkData	
User	A user who had registered for a LinkData account	
Link	**Term**	**Definition**
Data(new) → Data(old)	reuse	Create new Data by reusing existing Data
Data → User	contributed	The relationship between Existing Data and the user who created the Data
App(new) → App(old)	fork	Create a new App by reusing an existing App's program code
App → Data	load	Create an App by specifying some files as input from some particular Data
App → User	contributed	The relationship between an Existing App and the user who created the App
User(A) → User(B)	follow	User A follows user B to receive updates and information of evaluated Data and Apps by user B
User → Data	vote	A user gives a rating of Useful or Un-useful for considered Data
User → App	vote	A user gives a rating of Useful or Un-useful for a considered App

4) Application development support function: For application developers who want to use Data, the LinkData platform provides APIs which allow them to access to the contents of Data. Developers will be able to get the contents by five formats: TSV, RDF/Turtle, RDF/JSON, RDF/XML and RSS in their applications.

B. LinkDataApp as an application publishing platform

1) Creating application by editing sample program: We provide two ways to create new Apps: one is to select the "Create App" menu and the other is to go to LinkData's published Data page and create a new App for the data; a sample program of JavaScript is automatically generated when a User selects a file from published Data as an input and creates a new App. The User can edit the sample program on a web browser to develop an original App. Anyone accessing to the published App page will be able to execute and download the App.

2) Forking application to publish as a new one: Users can publish new Apps by forking any App created by others. When a User selects the "Fork App" menu or goes to a published App page, click the "Fork this app as your new one" button to open the program editor. After modification, the program can be published as a new App.

3) Changing input files to create a new application: When a User forks an App, the Input Data control system allows the user to control which LinkData input is loaded. A tagging system is provided to distinguish multiple files which might be referenced by an App. By changing the input data, even a non-programmer can add new functionality to the App.

III. METHODS

A. Entities and Links of LinkData concepts

Our combined platforms use three entities: Data, App and User. Data is a single data set which has been published by one or more Users of LinkData. It must have at least one file which is uploaded by User. App is a single JavaScript application which has been published by a User in LinkDataApp. It must load at least one file from Data. User is a person who had registered for as a user of the platforms. The relationships among entities are described as eight links shown in table 1. A link relationship represents the graph association from one entity node to another by which various metrics of value can be assigned to the recipient node because of the association. The metric value of each type of link and the count of these links are used according to an algorithm to assign a usability value.

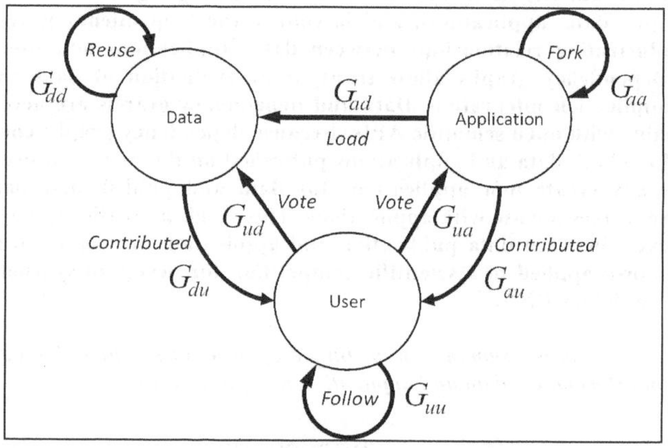

Fig. 1. **Dependency graph for usability analysis**

Three types of nodes: data, application and user, and eight types of links: Gdd, Gaa, Guu, Gad, Gud, Gua, Gdu and Gau are shown in the figure.

- Gdd is a graph connecting a data set to another data set that reuses the same data template or schema.
- Gaa is a graph connecting an application to another forked or modified application.
- Guu is a graph connecting a user who is following another user.
- Gad is a graph connecting a data set to an application loaded or used by that application.
- Gud is a graph connecting a user to a data set which is rated as "useful" or "un-useful" by the user.
- Gua is a graph connecting a user to an application which is rated by the user.
- Gdu is a graph connecting a data set to a user which is contributed by the user.
- Gad is a graph connecting an application to a user which is contributed by the user.

For the link new Data to old Data, a link termed "reuse," will be generated when a User creates new Data by reusing an existing schema from the old Data. The link Data to User, termed "contributed", will be generated when a User creates any Data. The link new App to old App, termed "fork", will be generated when a User creates a new App by reusing an existing App's program code. The link App to Data, termed "load", will be generated when a User creates a new App by specifying some files as input from some particular Data or loads some files in his/her existing App. The link User to User, termed "follow", will be generated when a User follows another User. For example, if User A follows User B, User A can receive updates about User B's Data or App and information about evaluated Data and Apps by User B. The links User to Data and User to App, termed "vote", will be generated when a user browses a Data or an App and gives rating of Useful or Un-useful for the considered Data or App. Dependency Graph for calculating Usability Scores.

B. *Dependecy Graph for calculating Usability scores*

In a dependency graph, the relationship between data and application make up the Utility portion of the graph measuring effectiveness of loading, data and data template reuse, and application forking (cloning and modification) in the creation of information. Three types of nodes: data, application and user, and eight types of links: Gdd, Gaa, Guu, Gad, Gud, Gua, Gdu and Gau are shown in Fig. 1. All the dependency graphs are downloadable from the LinkData.org APIs.

```
[API-TSV]
http://linkdata.org/api/1/graph/reuse_tsv.txt
http://linkdata.org/api/1/graph/fork_tsv.txt
http://linkdata.org/api/1/graph/load_tsv.txt
http://linkdata.org/api/1/graph/follow_tsv.txt
http://linkdata.org/api/1/graph/vote_data_tsv.txt
http://linkdata.org/api/1/graph/vote_app_tsv.txt

[API-JSON]
http://linkdata.org/api/1/graph/reuse_rdf.json
http://linkdata.org/api/1/graph/fork_rdf.json
http://linkdata.org/api/1/graph/load_rdf.json
http://linkdata.org/api/1/graph/follow_rdf.json
http://linkdata.org/api/1/graph/vote_data_rdf.json
http://linkdata.org/api/1/graph/vote_app_rdf.json
```

IV. Results and Discussion

A. *Count of relationships among three entities indicates creative synergy cycle*

LinkData hosts 557 datasets and 260 applications as of March, 2013. Datasets contain 350 public, 40 limited, and 162 private. Applications contain 160 public, 55 limited, and 45 private. There are a large number of Load (App to Data) relationships indicating Apps created by specifying some files as input from some particular Data (Table 2). There are also many Fork (App to App) relationships representing applications created by re-using program code from another application. In contrast, there are a few Reuse (Data to Data) classified relationships of new data created by using the template from another data set. It is thus clear that there is a stronger synergy cycle between data resources and applications than "in data" (between data and data). In other words, this indicates that a platform which has both capabilities of publishing data resources and creating applications has higher creativity than one having only one capability of data resource creation.

TABLE II. Count of relationships among data resources, applications and users in LinkData

Kind of relationship	Count
Load (App to Data)	166
Fork (App to App)	137
Reuse (Data to Data)	39
Follow (User to User)	52
Vote (User to Data)	244
Vote (User to App)	89

LinkData provides a public place to publish and analyze data. Hosting both data and apps together promotes useful public RDF data exchange between fields and the creation of new interdisciplinary fields. This spreads technology for scientific data to other fields, and educates about RDF techniques for any field.

B. *Visualization of a creative synergy cycle between data publication and application development*

Biological data analysis is one of the most important domains of applications of LOD in science. Fig. 2 shows an app called "Interactive Gene Association Matrix" for publishing a research result visualizing research data with Linkdata.org, where association analysis of two elements using a Venn diagram indicates how these elements associate or exclude each other. Tables and diagrams of co-localization of transcription factors and conservation between different species provide unbiased views of overlap or exclusion between two conditions. However, if the number of compared elements grows it could become too complex to see which items correlate well and which ones do not, so a comprehensive and interactive visualization tool should help researchers summarize their data and provide an overall view of their dataset.

The Interactive Gene Association Matrix runs on the LinkData web platform requiring no software installation. Researchers store their own association tables in LinkData and obtain automatically clustered matrix diagrams and Venn diagrams having statistical evaluation using hypergeometric distribution. The implementation shown indicates a blue (positively correlating) or red (negatively correlating) cell for each combination of two elements. Color intensity represents logarithm of odds ratio, and statistical significance can also be incorporated into the matrix as cells are masked in gray when the displayed overlap is insignificant. The diagram responds to

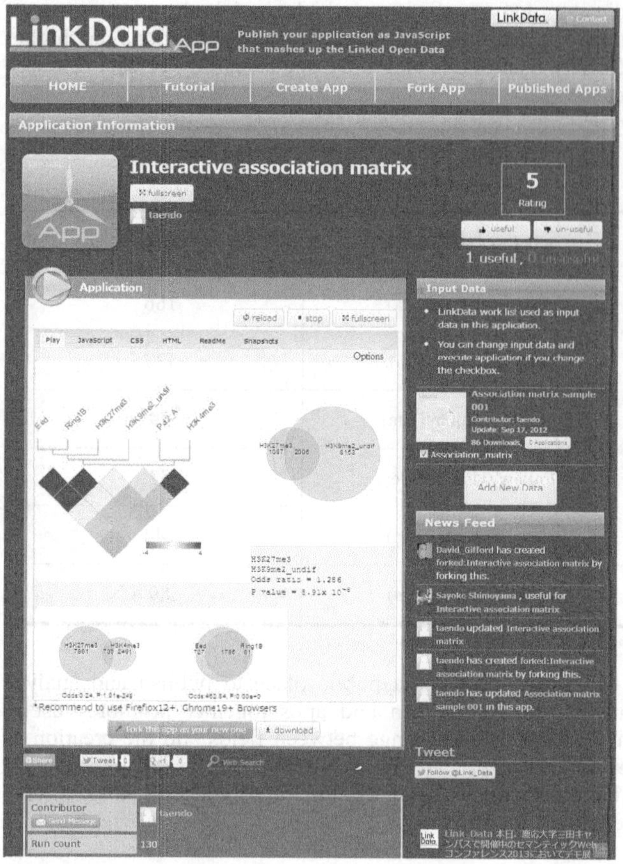

Fig. 2. **Interactive association matrix Application created on LinkDataApp** http://app.linkdata.org/run/app1s64i

a user's cursor moves and Venn diagram would be shown in right panel indicating statistical significance and raw odds ratio. Preferred Venn diagrams can be saved below when a cell is clicked to compare with overlap of other elements.

The matrix in Fig. 2 is made using epigenetic marks of transcription start sites of genes in mouse embryonic stem cells. This tool is not limited to gene by gene analysis, and can also be applied to any type of datasets if 2x2 contingency tables are available. The application can interpret RDF of data uploaded on LinkData. LinkDataApp allows all users to fork the application so that modified versions can have differences such as color representation and clustering algorithms. For example, it may be possible to compare various x and y elements for other species as well. The LinkData platform is very flexible for recombining different datasets as well as modifying the programming in LinkDataApp according to researchers' needs; and thus reuse of data and applications are observed as shown in Fig. 3.

C. *Rating data and apps based on the dependency graphs*

The dependency graph allows users to dynamically contribute to and benefit from an automated rating of both data and applications. The usability analysis score LinkData.org displays (Fig. 2 upper right) is calculated based on the dependency graphs to rank highly useful data and applications, so that the scores motivate users to release and update their data and applications, and trust other's open data. The core version of this rating system combines various works rating parameters as follows:

Rating published data resources + applications

In this type of rating, a user "votes" by using their judgment of the usability of the application. (Fig. 5) Users click a "useful" or "un-useful" button for positive or negative rating.

Rating for a LinkData work （LinkData)

Score = Useful count - Un-useful count + App count

This rating metric also integrates an indication of the App count measuring the number of apps using a data resource.

Rating for an Application （LinkDataApp)

Score = Useful count - Un-useful count + Fork count

An application's ranking also benefits from how many other applications have been generated as modified "forked" versions created by using the program code of another app.

For example in Fig. 2 and Fig. 3 application app1s69i is a fork of app1s64i. App1s69i loaded 2 data sources, contributed 1 time for a rank of just 3. App1s64i loads 1 data source, was contributed 1 time, and as well was forked 2 times and voted for 1 time to give a total rating of 5. In this fashion each app, dataset and user can be compared for total activity and usefulness in turn, as shown in Fig. 4.

D. *Application to a Scientific Competition showing creative synergy cycle on a massive scale*

For the synthetic biology competition GenoCon2 (http://genocon.org) [1], we challenged participants to design novel regulatory DNA for controlling gene expression in the thale cress plant *Arabidopsis thaliana*. Participant DNA designs will be synthesized and tested for tissue and time specificity in a real plant. To allow non-experts an opportunity for DNA design we built a computer aided design tool on the LinkData platform, called PromoterCAD (Fig. 5).

Using PromoterCAD function modules, genes with the desired properties can be found and mined for regulatory motifs. These are introduced into the synthetic promoter by user choice of regulatory position. Repeating this process can create complex regulation at the promoter. Finally, the DNA design is exported for error and safety checking, DNA synthesis, and experimental characterization.

Using PromoterCAD function modules, genes with the desired properties can be found and mined for regulatory motifs. These are introduced into the synthetic promoter by user choice of regulatory position. Repeating this process can create complex regulation at the promoter. Finally, the DNA design is exported for error and safety checking, DNA synthesis, and experimental characterization.

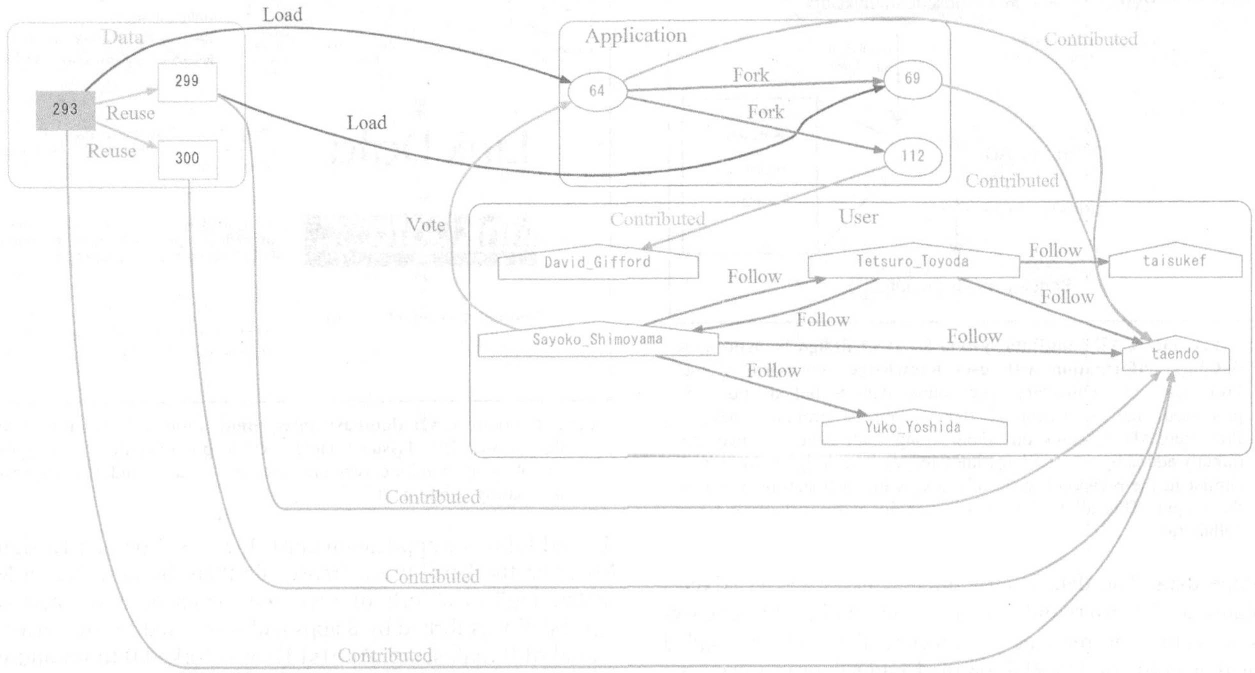

Fig. 3. **An example of dependency graph among Data, Apps and Users.** Dark Green edges indicate Data to Data **reuse** where a new data resource is published using a template of data published on LinkData, Red edges indicate Data to App **loading** in which a new application is created for data published on LinkData, Blue edges indicate App to App **forking** where new application is created by using program code of application created on LinkData. Bright green indicates User ownership **contribution** of a Data-set or an App. Grey edges indicate **votes** to rate various applications by users, and **following** of other users to receive updates of their activity and evaluations of their works.

PromoterCAD rests on a rich set of high throughput microarray and DNA sequence data containing over one million measurements and annotations of 20,000 genes. These were uploaded to LinkData as a series of data mashup tables and data rank lists (Fig. 6). Where other DNA design tools act as sequence editors with DNA specific functions, PromoterCAD is able to pull sequence data directly from the data sources in the LinkData system, guided by the menu-driven interface. PromoterCAD allows users to quickly perform advanced data queries, retrieve useful sequences, and organize them into their promoter sequence designs.

PromoterCAD also allows users to add their own knowledge of regulatory sequence data. Users may have literature knowledge of useful DNA sequences, so PromoterCAD allows these to be typed in and manipulated in the same manner as sequences retrieved from the LinkData sources. For example, one team of GenoCon2 participants introduced a DNA sequence that had been experimentally confirmed to confer dark inducibility to a plant gene. This sequence was combined with the LinkData to generate a DNA design they predicted to allow gene expression only in the flowering tissue of the plant, and only at night. In this way, PromoterCAD and LinkData allow expert users to combine their biological knowledge along with data mining operations from the LinkData sources.

The LinkData system provides code extensibility to PromoterCAD. With the forking function, users can write their own JavaScript data mining modules to PromoterCAD, and draw upon the rich linked data in new ways. For example, one participant in GenoCon2 modified a PromoterCAD function to display the top 10 expressing genes in a specific plant tissue. Other GenoCon2 participants used this module, and the forked utility has since been merged back into the main PromoterCAD functionality.

The architecture of PromoterCAD allows new LinkData sources to be added without any direct code modification. The LinkData forking system includes a flexible "Input Data" loading system. This allows users to control the LinkData that gets used for the PromoterCAD data mining tools. In a series of tutorials (http://promotercad.org), we clearly document how users can make their own LinkData tables and register them into forked versions of PromoterCAD. Examples are provided which explain how to add different types of experimental and

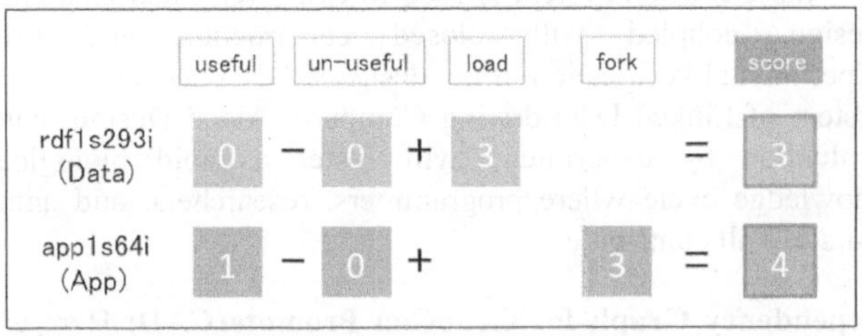

Fig. 4. **Example of Calculating a score** that integrates several Data and Application activity and User rating ranking score.

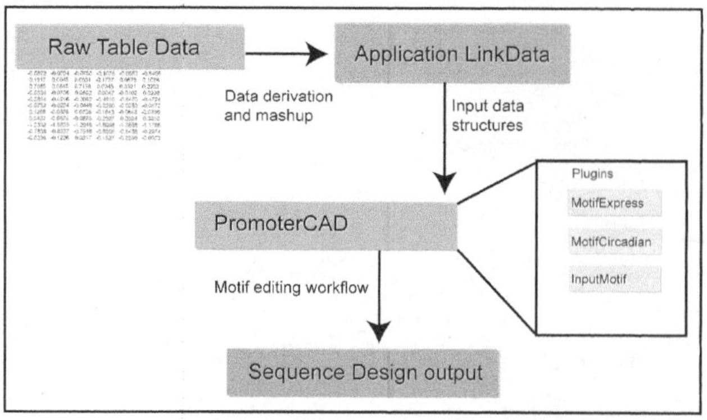

Fig. 5. **PromoterCAD LinkData system for DNA design incorporates database information with user knowledge** Overview of the PromoterCAD architecture. The source data is linked and then processed into a system of data suited to promoter design. PromoterCAD accesses this data, along with data that may be directly added by the user (user knowledge). The design workflow is similar to the revision history of a text, with each step recorded in the output. This allows for easy checking of the design and for collaboration.

sequence data. The data is structured with LinkData (Excel) templates so that users only need to copy and paste gene expression values or regulatory sequence lists. The uploaded data is then converted to RDF on the LinkData.org server. This function is intended to allow scientists who are not programmers to add their own databases to PromoterCAD. By replacing all of the data tables, a user could adapt PromoterCAD to design regulatory DNA in other organisms such as mouse, human, or bacteria.

PromoterCAD is also a learning tool. A special LinkData file contains pointers to external links, including the original data sources. This links appear directly in PromoterCAD web interface, so that users can quickly obtain more information about a particular gene or sequence. These include links to gene expression visualization websites such as the "electronic fluorescent pictogram" browser for *Arabidopsis* [2] and HanaDB [3]. This allows users to see illustrations of the gene expression patterns, which are presented in PromoterCAD as Highchart plots (http://www.highcharts.com).

Powerful tooltip functionality allows all LinkData sources to be annotated in a separate tooltip table. This provides guidance for the users who might not have familiarity with gene expression microarray data or promoter analysis. Furthermore, the tooltip files can be easily modified to create interactive tutorials for guiding users in promoter design.

This GenoCon system is used to empower Open Genomic Design, coupled with closed construction and safe experimental verification of the designed DNA sequences. The system of Linked Data driving Computer Aided Design, with evaluation by experiment, will foster a rapid biological knowledge cycle where programmers, researchers, and amateurs can all contribute.

Dependency Graph for GenoCon PromoterCAD: Here we show the cycle enhancing synergistic collaboration in this web-based scientific competition for synthetic biology promoter design. (Fig. 7) For example in Fig. 7 and Fig. 8 highly voted

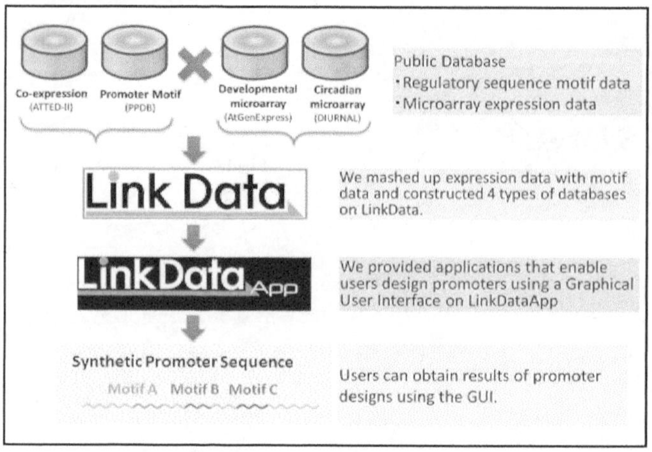

Fig. 6. **PromoterCAD database integration.** PromoterCAD uses several data sources for Tissue / Time specific promoter design. 4 types of sample data combine two promoter motif data, and two expression microarray experiments.

for and followed application app1s137i "A Promoter Design to Maintain the Fertility of Transgenic Plant by new Plugin MotifRanking" is a fork of app1s94i GenoCon PromoterCAD. App1s94i was forked by 8 apps and was voted for by 1 user for a total of 9 rank score. App1s137i was forked 0 times and was voted for by 5 users for a rank score of 5. In this fashion each app can be compared for total activity and usefulness in turn.

Contest Activity: The GenoCon2 promoter design contest generated active user groups and over 40 international submissions including from the USA, Egypt and Japan. Key users cooperated to create original designs that were modified and possibly improved by other users. Team collaboration was aided by the open nature of the design platform, and 13 promoter designs are being considered for final construction in transgenic plants. Application to further design challenge projects for other organisms is also planned.

V. Conclusions

Ease of generation of new applications on top of existing data is a practical benefit for scientists, with faster development making it potentially easy for other scientists to jump in at any step of a research process and test pre-existing data analysis, and more easily recreate to check what the original researcher has done. A major benefit of the LinkData platform for biological research is that unique analysis modules and database structures could possibly be reused for future and different organism related research.

Because dependency graphs combine both data and applications published on the platform, users easily create new applications for data and publish new data resources for use with applications. This yields a creative synergy cycle between data publication and application development. As a future plan we propose the use of the LinkData.org integrated database/application concept including dependency graphs to be applied for CKAN and other major repositories.

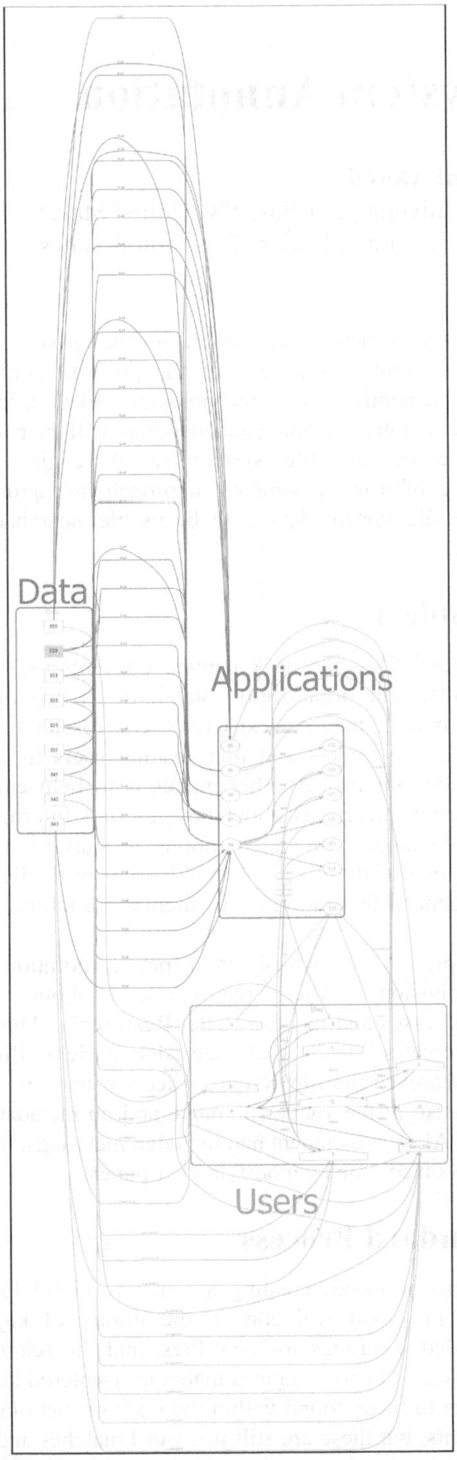

Fig. 7. **Dependency graph of the PromoterCAD application on LinkData.** This graph shows the interaction between the LinkData (Green color box), the Apps (Blue color box), and the Users (Grey color box). Red lines show the loading, creation of apps by specifying some particular Data . Blue lines indicate the forking of an App into a new App. Green lines show which users have created each Data or App. The Grey lines indicate the interest expressed in each Data, App or User by the Users. In this graph highly rated and followed application app1s137i is a fork of app1s94i which is ranked higher.

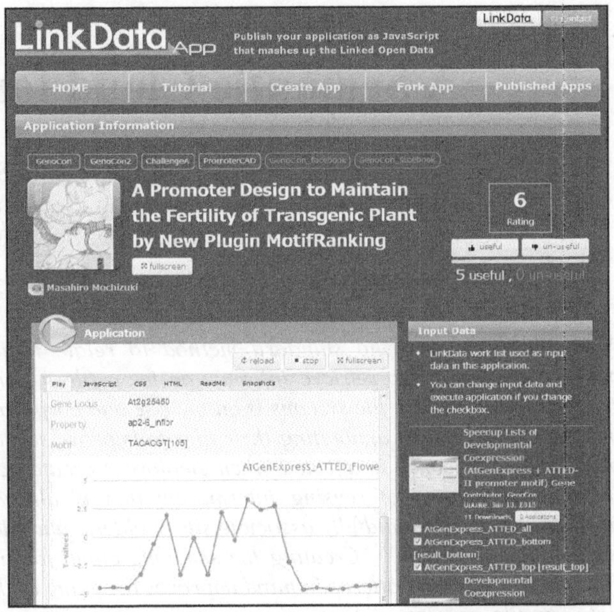

Fig. 8. **LinkData Application app1s137i showing usability ranking and user voting buttons on top right.** http://app.linkdata.org/app/app1s137i

ACKNOWLEDGEMENT

We would like to acknowledge: Dr. Takaho Endo for creating biological visualization tool on LinkDataApp. Ms. Yuko Yoshida for development of converter and valuable discussion. Dr. Shuji Kawaguchi for giving advice on score calculation. Dr. Koro Nishikata for testing LinkData. Dr. Masahiro Mochizuki for testing and adding the MotifRanking tool. Mr. Chanaka Perera, Mr. Uditha Punchihewa, Mr. Gayan Hewathanthri, Mr. Hiroaki Osada, Mr. Kazuro Fukuhara and Mr. Kiyoshi Mizumoto (Axiohelix Co., Ltd.) for web application and LinkData development. The committee of Linked Open Data Challenge Japan for continuing interest and encouragement.

This work was supported by the National Bioscience Database Center (NBDC) of the Japan Science and Technology Agency (JST).

REFERENCES

[1] T. Toyoda, et al.: "Methods for Open Innovation on a Genome – Design Platform Associating Scientific, Commercial, and Educational Communities in Synthetic Biology," Methods in Enzymology., Vol. 498, 189-203, (2011)

[2] D. Winter, Ben Vinegar, H. Nahal, R. Ammar, G. V. Wilson, and N. J. Provart, "An 'Electronic Fluorescent Pictograph' Browser for Exploring and Analyzing Large-Scale Biological Data Sets," PLoS ONE, vol. 2, no. 8, p. e718, Aug. 2007.

[3] K. Hanada, M. Higuchi-Takeuchi, M. Okamoto, T. Yoshizumi, M. Shimizu, K. Nakaminami, R. Nishi, C. Ohashi, K. Iida, M. Tanaka, Y. Horii, M. Kawashima, K. Matsui, T. Toyoda, K. Shinozaki, M. Seki, and M. Matsui, "Small open reading frames associated with morphogenesis are hidden in plant genomes.," Proc Natl Acad Sci USA, Jan. 2013.

A Semantic Cloud for File System Annotation

Tyronda Strong[1], **Pavani Akundi**[2]
[1]Computer Science and Engineering, Southern Methodist University, Dallas, TX, United States
[2]Computer Science and Engineering, Southern Methodist University, Dallas, TX, United States

Abstract - *There is no standard method to relate topics between documents to retrieve information for a file system. The amount of data in file systems is on the rise and corporate intranets benefit from annotating their files to improve search performance. Search is affected when employees create new information instead of reusing information that is already available or do not mindfully associate sites, folders, and files within the file system. Creating the semantic cloud for file systems with search patterns in mind improves the value of the data on file servers. Semantic annotation and meta-tags methods support the creation of networks of files towards information relevancy for meaningful searches.*

Keywords: File systems, meta-data, meta-tag, RDF, semantic annotation, semantic cloud

1 Introduction

Web standards, like schema.org, [1] (adopted by Google, Bing, Yahoo, and Yandex) have been helpful in considering annotation of metadata for databases and file systems that are within private networks such as schools and corporations. In a database, content may need metadata annotation or tags to make it machine readable; however, the extraction, analysis, and editing process for annotation is manual. Annotated files allow querying, searching, and reporting of patterns within a dataset, but will be a full time job for anyone attempting to enforce tagging on all the files in their organization. File systems are typically unstructured, without metadata, and do not have a pre-defined data model for searching and organizing which contribute to the challenges involved in structuring files with annotation.

Web search engines have been the primary focus of structuring data, but intranet environments within corporations lack robust search capabilities [2]. Corporate file systems are nonrepresentational file stores of numerous file types and information. Creating, storing, and accessing files in an organization will vary and grow based on the needs of users, teams, and departments. As these data collections grow, improving data processing and search methods is important.

This paper proposes a semantic cloud to configure a file system for search. Although, search may already be an available function in many applications and browsers, defining a standard protocol will assist all users innately manage the company file structure and assist in the greater goal of building an information network for projects and groups. Utilizing semantic web technologies like information extraction, annotation, and data mapping will help create a semantic cloud for file system search engines. The significance of using a semantic approach in capturing and organizing file system data is to be usable, searchable, and modifiable.

2 Problem

Folders and files may lack naming conventions, metadata requirements, and organization standards. Configuration guidelines may or may not exist for users to reference at the time they create folders and files leading users to make up their own definitions. Another matter is to help employees make informed decisions about how to find information in historical documents instead of opting to start from scratch [3]. Any one of these actions could result in duplication of work and general frustration with searching for a file.

For example, Alice works for a pet corporation canine research division. Alice creates File 1 about Labrador retriever illnesses and names it, "Pet Research". Three years later, Bob creates File 2 called "Labrador Retriever Illnesses". When he searched the file system, Alice's paper could not be found because of the vague file name and no metadata about the file. If Alice's document had included meta-tags, then Bob could have saved time by modifying her paper.

3 Standard Process

This paper proposes creating a semantic cloud for a file system. The cloud will contain the library of key-terms, recommended meta-tags for new files, and the relationships between files. Search engines match user-entered keywords and phrases to those found within the texts or meta-tag fields of documents, but these are still just word matches and do not necessarily go after the meaning of a document [4].

Windows search returns numerous files that do not meet the intent of the search. In previous versions of Microsoft Office, the search capability was not as robust as a web search engines like Google. When users searched for specific terms the results were too numerous or vague to be useful. With Windows 7, Office now has the ability to search tags and by utilizing tags in our process users will be able to find the data they are looking for and then they will not create new documents with repetitive information.

Linking data semantically gives users the ability to perform a meaningful search. Instead of trying to think of creative search terms, they will have a finite set of keywords to annotate their documents via a standard library of key terms. This paper proposes improving key word searches by annotating new files using semantic tagging.

The semantic cloud covers all the relationships for every entity existing in a file system. In the semantic cloud topics are key words and categories are relationships. Consider the cloud to exist as a layer above the file system with pointers from the layer to the file. This eliminates restructuring the file system and downtime required to index the search libraries.

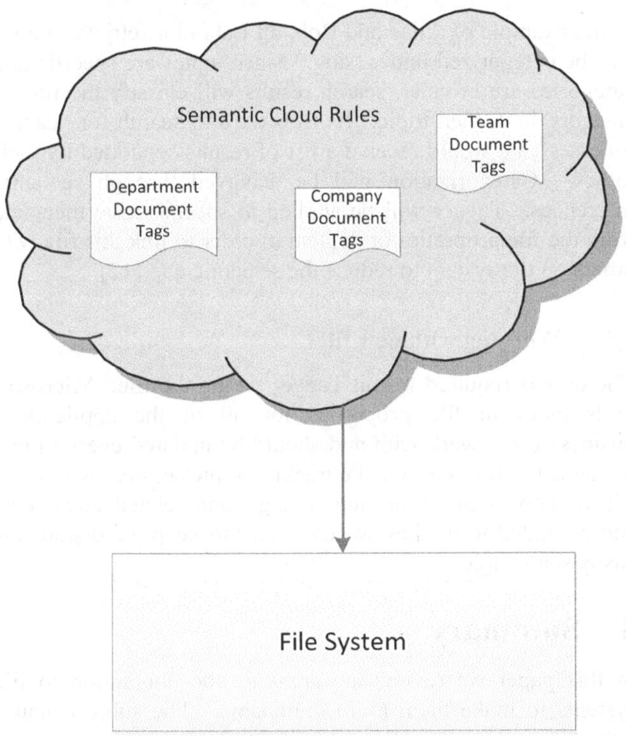

Fig.1. File System Semantic Cloud

Each of the following tasks contributes to the development of the standard key term library.

1. Classify Topics
2. Create Categories
3. Reduce redundancies

This is an iterative process and as more information is gathered, specifics are uncovered, and similarities are found, the system details may need to be adjusted in the semantic cloud. A group of systems engineers who understand how the system is currently organized will be responsible for creating and maintaining the semantic cloud.

3.1 Classify Topics

3.1.1 Build the system diagram and map.

The system diagram displays the file system structure and the map is the starting point for the development of the semantic cloud. Building the system diagram allows the system engineers to understand the topics. Based on the diagram classify content by companies, departments, and individual teams to create topic maps. Topics will represent tags in the key term library. Identifying links between tags will help identify similarities across the domain and condense topics where suitable. In the example, Alice's file would be classified under the topic "research".

3.2 Classifying metadata in existing files

Use extraction techniques to discover topics, relationships, and new or existing metadata.

3.2.1 Information Extraction

Information Extraction's is used to extract specific information from semi-structured and unstructured text according to a pre-defined template [Source: Wen-Jie Li. Ontology-based Drug Product Information Extraction System.] Extracting data using natural language processing (NLP) and pre-defined or learned rules converts some of the information to "explicit metadata"[2]. Using NLP, the rules must cover such things as parts-of-speech, language specific grammar rules, and sentence structure. Finally, NLP should extract meaning from this data [5]. The problem with NLP is that in spite of these rules, it is tedious to analyze the vague descriptions without having subject matter knowledge of the content or a solid grasp of the rule sets applied to the metadata.

3.2.2 Data Mining

Data mining plays an important role in defining search. The application of algorithms can assist in pairing data to its basic elements to define relationships [6]. Using association rules and similarity algorithms can support identifying the commonalities between related nodes in the semantic cloud and automate this solution.

Using the techniques from information extraction and data mining, a tag extraction tool (Tagger) is created to extract the relevant tags from a file to incorporate into the key term library. The subject matter experts will be consulted to help classify the documents into the correct areas and eliminate terms. After performing the techniques on Alice's file, the keywords are "illnesses", "Labrador retriever", and "training". The subject matter experts determine that training is not a key term.

3.3 Key Term Library

We model the key-term library with the resource description framework (RDF) and XML[7] [8] to represent linked data between files with similar tags. RDF triples are simple to generate from a baseline of key-terms that may be loosely documented in an unformatted text file and extensible enough to search with SPARQL Protocol and RDF Query Language (SPARQL) [9]. The Jena framework built on Java consists of a number of tools specifically aimed at representing link data on the web [10]. Although file systems and corporate networks may not necessarily have a web presence, this paper proposes that defining relationships between files is valuable to allow for a better understanding of the corporate information network as a whole and in terms of its unique areas. We use RDF triples to document key-terms allows semantic search patterns to arise from the rules and definitions.

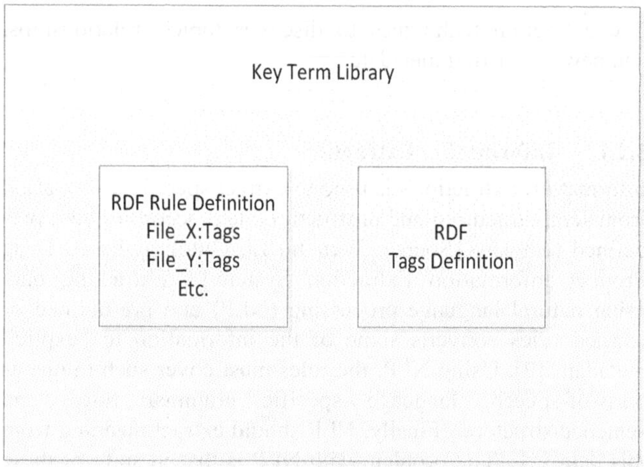

Fig.2. Key Term RDF files

RDF may be expressed using the Extensible Markup Language (XML) called RDF/XML or in a more compact notation called turtle. Figure 3 illustrates a RDF/XML description of the statement about the Pet Corporation.

```
@prefix foaf:
<http://xmlns.com/foaf/0.1/> .
@prefix : <http://Pet_Shop>.
<rdf:Description
rdf:about="http://Pet_Shop/labrador">
<dc:title>Canine Illness</dc:title>
<rdf:type
rdf:resource="http://xmlns.com/foaf/sp
ec/Document"/>
<dc:creator
rdf:resource="http://Pet_Shop/alice"/>
</rdf:Description>
```

Fig. 3. A RDF/XML example

In addition to RDF/XML the RDF/turtle notation [11] provides a more compact way to represent RDF triples. Prefixes and qualified names (qnames) allow a user to only provide a namespace prefix and identifier to describe each triple. Figure 4 illustrates the same data using RDF/turtle.

```
@prefix foaf:
<http://xmlns.com/foaf/0.1/> .
@prefix : <http://Pet_Shop/> .
:canine_research dc:creator :alice .
:canine_research a foaf:Document .
:canine_research dc:title "Canine
Illnesses" .
```

Fig. 4. A RDF/turtle example

3.4 Creating Categories and reduce redundancies

In the example of Alice and Bob, all Labrador retriever topics will be categorized under "dog." Since topics are specific and categories are broader, search results will classify the file by category first, then topic. If Bob were to search for "canine illnesses", he would receive a list of results separated by their topics. Categorization will be achieved through semantic inferences. Tagger will be applied to specify basic metadata from the file properties or content in order to link this file with others on the system to reduce the semantic gap [12].

3.5 Working with new files

The user is required to run Tagger saving the file. Microsoft tools maintain file properties for all of the applications business users work with and should be updated every time a document is revised to make tracking topics easier. Microsoft file properties like title, author, tags, and related documents can be added to the key words library to keep the documents easily searchable.

4 Summary

In this paper we review the areas to add annotation to file systems to make them more searchable. The subject matter experts for an organization will need to perform the analysis to define the acceptable metadata properties and promote semantic annotation across new and existing files for a semantic cloud. Maintaining relationships between historical documentation and minimizing rework offer opportunities despite these challenges.

Each organizations implementation of this semantic cloud will be tailored to their file system and users. Further research will delve into the actual implementation of a search, tag extraction and annotation tools that will complement the standard presented in this paper.

5 References

[1] (February 2). *What is Schema.org?* Available: http://schema.org/

[2] F. Bry, A. Kohn, and A. Manta, "Semantic search on unstructured data: explicit knowledge through data recycling," *International Journal on Semantic Web and Information Systems,* vol. 6, p. 17+, 2010 April-June 2010.

[3] R. Rao, "From unstructured data to actionable intelligence," *IT Professional,* vol. 5, pp. 29-35, 2003.

[4] H. Heather, "How SEMANTIC TAGGING Increases Findability," *EContent,* vol. 31, pp. 38-43, 2008.

[5] P. M. Nadkarni, L. Ohno-Machado, and W. W. Chapman, "Natural language processing: an introduction," *Journal of the American Medical Informatics Association : JAMIA,* vol. 18, pp. 544-51, 09/01 2011.

[6] P. Klinov and L. J. Mazlack, "Granulating semantic web ontologies," in *Granular Computing, 2006 IEEE International Conference on*, 2006, pp. 431-434.

[7] W3C. *RDF Primer*. Available: http://www.w3.org/TR/2004/REC-rdf-primer-20040210/

[8] W3C. (March 2013). *RDF/XML Syntax*. Available: http://www.w3.org/TR/rdf-syntax-grammar/

[9] B. DuCharme, *Learning SPARQL*: O'Rielly Media.

[10] A. Jena. (March 6). *Apache Jena*. Available: http://jena.apache.org/

[11] "Turtle."

[12] P. M. K. Gordon, K. Barker, and C. W. Sensen, "Programming-by-Example Meets the Semantic Web: Using Ontologies and Web Services to Close the Semantic Gap," in *Visual Languages and Human-Centric Computing (VL/HCC), 2010 IEEE Symposium on*, 2010, pp. 133-140.

Constructing a Semantic-Based Image Retrieving system – Image Semantic Searching System (ISSS)

Yi Liu[1], Peiyi Xiao[1], and Michael C. Wimberly[2]
[1]Dept. of Electrical Engineering and Computer Science, South Dakota State University, Brookings, USA
[2]GISc Center of Excellence, South Dakota State University, Brookings, USA

Abstract - *Because of the great volume of image resources produced and gathered on the web for public browsing, image retrieving tools and systems play an important role for users in retrieving image resources. A novel image retrieving system, the Image Semantic Search System (ISSS), was designed and implemented based on semantic web concepts and techniques. The paper illustrates the methodology for designing the sematic search system to provide user friendly interfaces and relevant searching results. The paper also presents the architectural design and implementation of the system and uses a case study to demonstrate the application of ISSS.*

Keywords: semantic web; image search system; web application

1 Introduction

Due to the large volume image resources produced and gathered on the internet, it becomes difficult for end users to retrieve desired resources. Although numerous of image retrieving systems have been developed based on different methodologies, there are still some key problems that have not been adequately resolved. For example, users typically take too many responsibilities for retrieving relevant results. Therefore, in order to provide a good searching experience to the users, there is a need for developing more result relevant and user friendly image retrieving systems.

A prevailing response to this need is semantic-based image retrieving systems. Semantic-based approaches extract the semantic meaning of the image resources using Semantic Web [1] techniques to interpret both the resources and the users in order to reduce users' responsibilities and always provide users with relevant results.

This research aims to construct a novel semantic-based image retrieval system *Image Semantic Searching System* (ISSS) to provide users better experience on searching images. The ISSS is designed for both image seekers, who search for the images, and image producers, who generate or publish the images. For the image seekers, ISSS should have simple and easy-to-use interfaces and always provide relevant results to users without any duplicated or wasted effort. For the image producers, ISSS should have user friendly interfaces and should support reusability in other websites.

Below lists the objectives for the design of ISSS.

Objective 1: The system should provide user friendly interfaces for both image seekers and image producers.

Objective 2: The system should always provide the most relevant results for image seekers.

For each search, the system will provide the most relevant result if it can be found; otherwise, it will return no result.

Objective 3: Although this image searching system was initially designed for searching map images stored in a web atlas, it should provide an easy way to make it reusable in other websites as an image search component.

The paper focuses on the construction of ISSS. Section 2 illustrates the background information that is used in ISSS. Section 3 illustrates the methodology of the design of the ISSS. Section 4 shows architectural design of the ISSS and Section 5 sketches the implementation. Section 6 demonstrates how to plug-in ISSS in a real world application. Section 7 summarizes and discusses the results.

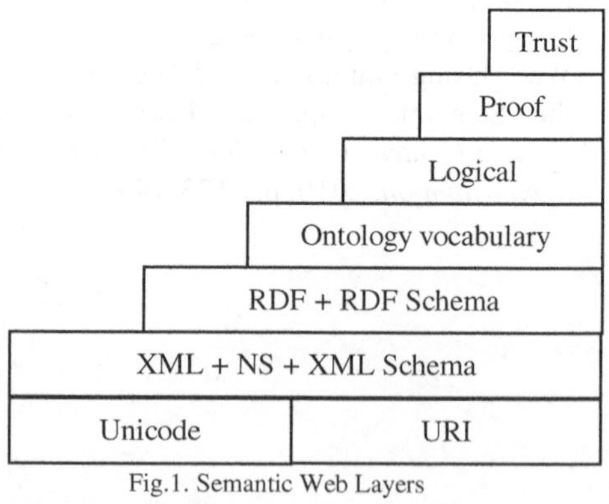

Fig.1. Semantic Web Layers

2 Background

2.1 Semantic web

The semantic web technique is adopted for developing the ISSS. The semantic web is used to help computers "understand" the information on the web so that they can support richer discovery, data integration, navigation and automation of tasks [2, 3].

The Semantic Web principles are implemented in the layers of web technologies and standards shown in Fig. 1[1]. The Unicode and Uniform Resource Identifier (URI) layer guarantees the international characters sets to be used to provide identical means for resources or objects. The XML layer ensures the Semantic Web definitions can be integrated with other XML based standards. The RDF and RDF Schema layers are responsible for describing each resource or object by make statements about the URI of resources. The Ontology layer defines the relationships between the different concepts of each vocabulary. The Logic layer enables the writing of rules while the Proof layer executes the rules and evaluates together with the Trust layer mechanism for applications whether to trust the given proof or not. At the present time, the Logic, Proof and Trust layers are still under development and have not yet been incorporated into the application.

2.2 Dublin Core

The Dublin Core metadata terms [4,5] are a set of vocabulary terms which can be used for the purposes of discovery and generic resource description. The terms can be used to describe a full range of web resources: video, images, web pages, and etc. The simple Dublin Core Metadata Element Set (DCMES) consists of 15 metadata elements [6]:

title	identifier	source	language	relation
coverage	rights	creator	subject	description
publisher	contributor	date	type	format

These metadata terms can represent the characteristics of each resource in different perspectives, and each resource can be described or organized around these terms. Based on different needs, terms from the set can be adopted to describe new resources, or the original term set can be extended to add more terms. For ISSS, we adopt title, subject, coverage, date, and format to describe image resources, and we rename them to be *theme, event, location, period* and *style,* respectively.

3 Methodology

In order to satisfy objective 2 to provide the most relevant results to image seekers, ISSS should interpret both users' input and resources correctly. We propose a methodology for describing resources, extracting information, organizing resource properties and inferring resources. The whole interpretation process, as shown in Fig. 2, is divided into three parts: resource description, information extraction, and resource inference.

3.1 Resource Description

One of the Semantic Web techniques, Resource Description Framework (RDF), is used to organize and describe resources thoroughly. For interpreting each resource effectively, a resource model with five basic properties (adoption of the Dublin core) – *theme, event, location, period* and *style* is designed and applied into RDF.

It is not reasonable to produce duplicated resources, so we assume that there are no duplicated resources in storage, which means that no two resources have identical properties. In this way, the properties make each resource unique and searchable. For example, a resource whose properties are West Nile Virus (theme), Incidence Rate (event), South Dakota (location), 2011 (period) and JPG (style) differs from another newly produced resource with the properties – West Nile Virus (theme), Incidence Rate (event), South Dakota (location), 2012 (period) and JPG (style). Even though they have similar properties, the difference of their period property makes them different and unique.

By applying the resource description model, each resource can be interpreted by checking and identifying all its associated properties. If all the properties of a resource are exactly match those a user indicates, then the resource is the user's wanted result. To get relevant results, interpreting only resources is not enough. It is not possible to match a resource without users' indication as reference. So, another important issue is how to interpret input from the users.

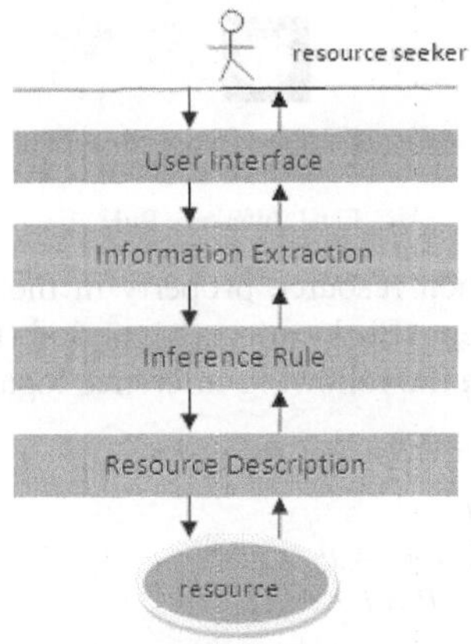

Fig. 2. Interpretation process

3.2 Information Extraction

Information Extraction is used to analyze user input and extracts useful information to find out users' target results. To avoid missing any useful information and provide flexibility of user input, the system extracts information in two different ways - Syntax Interpretation and Semantic Interpretation.

The syntactic styles of users' input can vary, based on different spelling habits. For example, "West Nile Virus" is treated as same as "WNV" or "West Nile." For interpreting a word or a phrase in different syntactic styles, it is necessary to collect and organize the different syntactic forms of that word or phrase. Another way to interpret a phrase or a word in a different syntax is to identify its misspelling forms. For example, a misspelled phrase "West Nile Virous" has explicit meaning of "West Nile Virus". Thus, organizing and identifying the misspelled phrases also facilitates interpreting user input. A Syntax Thesaurus is attached to the system to help the system identify user input in various syntactic forms. The Syntax Thesaurus organizes common words and their spelling and misspelling variations.

The Semantic Interpretation focuses on words' synonyms. The meaning of a word can be represented by identifying and interpreting its synonyms. For instance, "incidence rate" has the same meaning as "incidence proportion". Similar to the process of Syntax Interpretation, a Synonym Thesaurus is constructed to identify the synonyms of the core words used to describe a resource.

3.3 Inference Rule

An Inference Rule is the act of inferring the unknown information of a resource based on the interpreted information. Due to the large volume of resources that may accumulate in resource storage, we designed an Inference Rule for inferring the target resources by narrowing down the searching range purpose. Fig.3 shows the Inference Rule.

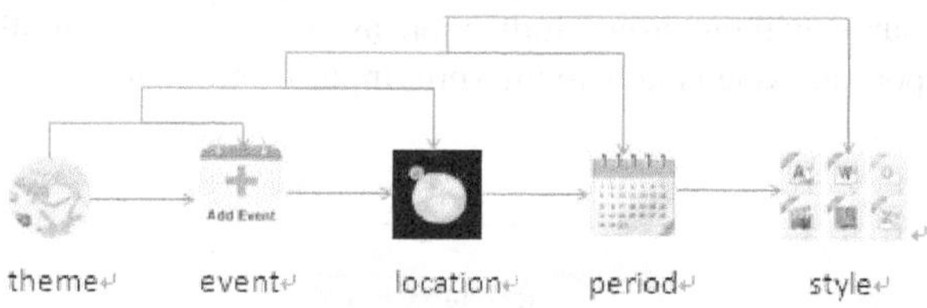

Fig.3. Inference Rule

Consider each resource property in the resource model as theme (T), event (E), location (L), period (P) and style (S), and then we have the following inference logic:

$T \rightarrow E$

$\neg T \rightarrow \neg E$

$(T \rightarrow E) \wedge T \rightarrow L$

$(T \rightarrow E) \rightarrow L \wedge T \wedge E \rightarrow P$

$((T \rightarrow E) \rightarrow L) \rightarrow P \wedge T \wedge E \wedge L \rightarrow S$

$(T \wedge \neg E) \rightarrow \neg L$

$(T \wedge E \wedge \neg L) \rightarrow \neg P$

$(T \wedge E \wedge P \wedge \neg E) \rightarrow \neg S$

$(T \rightarrow E) \wedge (E \rightarrow L) \rightarrow (T \rightarrow L)$

$(T \rightarrow E) \wedge (E \rightarrow L) \wedge (L \rightarrow P) \rightarrow (T \rightarrow P) \vee (E \rightarrow P)$

$(T \rightarrow E) \wedge (E \rightarrow L) \wedge (L \rightarrow P) \wedge (P \rightarrow S) \rightarrow (T \rightarrow S) \vee (E \rightarrow P) \vee (E \rightarrow S) \vee (L \rightarrow S)$

$(T \rightarrow E \wedge E \wedge P \wedge \neg E) \rightarrow \neg S$

A traditional method for inferring resource information is schematizing the content of Resource Description Framework (RDF) by using Resource Description Framework Schema (RDFS) and using RDF query language such as SPARQL [7] to parse the RDF and RDFS files to query and infer resource information. This requires the construction of a resource schema file and the annotation of the relationships between the information. In addition, an extra query language is needed for querying the resource description and resource description schema files. The query processes may be complicated and time consuming based on the construction and format of the parsed files. Our method focuses on constructing a resource information file, which is formatted automatically based on the Inference Rule when resources are generated. There is no need to construct a resource schema file, or use a query language and the associated query rule to get the information. Therefore, our method is more efficient and convenient compared to the traditional method.

4 Architectural Design of ISSS

The following assumptions are made to serve as the basis of the architectural design of ISSS.

(1) The resources include many different image types such as JPEG, PDF, PNG, KML, and KMZ and so on. The image resource is stored in the system and available for retrieval.

(2) Two different user interfaces are provided for two types of users – resource seekers and resource providers. Resource seekers search and view the resources stored in the system through a data reading interface, and resource providers generate the resource and store them in the system through a data providing interface.

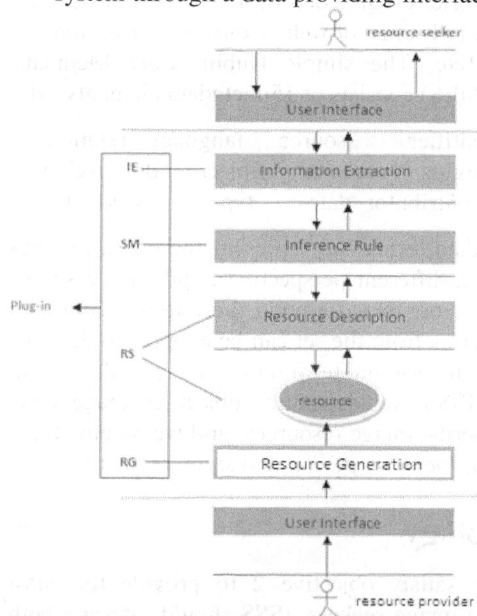

Fig. 4. ISSS Components

ISSS adopts the client-server architecture for the entire system. Resource seekers and resource providers are on the client side and they are provided user interfaces to interact with the server side. Components *Information Extraction (IE)*, *Search Engine (SE)*, *Resource Storage (RS)* and *Resource Generation (RG)*, are sitting on the server side to perform the tasks of storing resources, analyzing the resource seekers' inputs, and conducting searching.

Information Extraction (IE) Component

IE maps to Information Extraction that is described in the methodology. IE is responsible for collecting the resource seeker's input and extracting the semantic meaning of the input through the data reading interface. A Syntax Thesaurus and a Synonym Thesaurus are attached to the IE component to check and interpret the input information.

Resource Storage (RS) Component

RS maps to the Resource Description for storing all the resources and monitors the requests from other components. Each resource stored in RS is described and organized based on the applied Resource Description Model. RS also provides the functionality for retrieving resources from storage and sending them to other components. For example, RS will provide the requested resource to SE when it sends a request.

Search Engine (SE) Component

SE maps to Inference Rule for searching target resources. It carries users' input and accesses other components to query and check resources, and then provides resource properties information or searching results to users. Theme, event, location, period and style are used as the basic properties to describe each resource. The inference rule specified in section 3 is applied into SE for identifying the resource properties, checking the resource availability and reducing the target resource's range. SE communicates with IE and gets the extracted properties of the resources from it. With the known resource properties from IE, SE provides a user-friendly interface to get the unknown properties from the users through the interface. After all the properties are collected by SE, it interacts with the RS to query resources.

Resource Generation (RG) Component

RG allows the resource provider to generate resources and store them into the RS. The operations and interfaces of RG are provided in the resource generator view. It provides three operations, *addForResource(),addForSourceCheck()*and *addForThesaurus()*. After generators finish creating the resource, the operation *addForResource()* stores the created resource into RS, operation *addForSourceCheck()* puts the resource property information into the Inference Rule file, and *addForThesaurus()* sends the resource property synonym information to the Synonym Thesaurus.

Resource providers produce resources through the user interface provided by RG. RG communicates with RS and stores all the produced resources in RS. IE monitors users' searching requests and extracts the information from their input. It then contacts SE to send users' requests and the related data of resources. Finally, SE searches the resources and sends the requests to RS to retrieve and display the search result to users. Their interactions are illustrated in Fig.5.

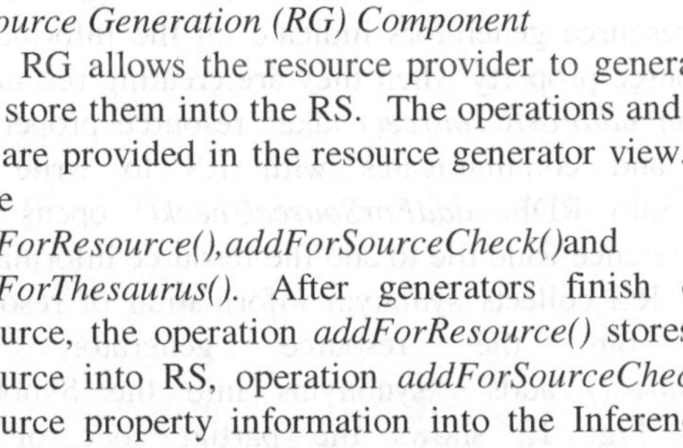

Fig.5. ISSS component interactions

5 Implementation

The server side of ISSS was coded in PHP 5[8]. The Client side scripts were developed in HTML for the structure of user interfaces, JavaScript and AJAX [9] for the interactions, and Cascading Style Sheets (CSS) [10] for adding styles to the web page layouts.

RDF and Inference Rule

All the resources are defined and stored in the RDF based on the applied Resource Description Model. In RDF, XML is used to express the resource information in form of triples: Subject-Property-Value. User defined tags are used in RDF to describe the attributes or characteristics of each resource. The name/link of each image resource is treated as the Subject. The property of description model is the Property, and the text content of the property is the Value. Fig. 6 shows an example of image resource description. Tag *<regardTo>* is for the property *Theme*, displayed is for *Event*, *<recoding>* is for *Period*, *<occurred>* is for *Location*, and *<madeInto>* is for *Style*. The inference rules for resource descriptions are stored in an inference rule file shown in Fig. 7.

```
<resource>
  <image id="0" name="Timeseries incidence rates from 2002-2011"
      link="/model/maps/asia_trip_n.kmz">
    <regardTo resource="west nile virus" />
    <displayed resource="incidence rate" />
    <recording resource="2002-2011" />
    <occurred resource="northern great plains" />
    <madeInto resource="kml" />
  </image>
</resource>
```

Fig. 6. A sample resource description with one piece of image resource

```
<?xml version="1.0" ?>
- <source>
  - <theme id="west nile virus">
    - <event id="incidence rate">
      - <area id="northern great plains">
        - <time id="2002-2011">
            <type id="kml" />
          </time>
        </area>
      </event>
    </theme>
  </source>
```

Fig. 7. Inference rule file

Implementation of Information Extraction (IE) Component

The main operation of the IE component is *extractProperties()*, which tries to extract all the properties information of resources. This operation includes several sub functions, each of which is for extracting one of the properties in the Resource Description Model. During information extraction, IE opens and parses the attached syntax and synonym thesauruses for the syntax and semantic interpretation. The thesauruses are well organized by using XML. Fig. 8 shows the partial codes of IE and Fig.9 and 10 show the partial content of the thesauruses.

```
class InformationExtraction
{ function extractProperties($content, $theme, $event,
      $location, $period, $style)
  { extractTheme();        extractEvent();        extractLocation();
    extractPeriod();       extractStyle();
  }
  ...
}
```

Fig. 8. Partial code of IE component

```
<?xml version="1.0"?>
<syntax from="WIKI MISSPELLING DATABASE">
 <aFile commnet="all the words start with alphabet-a">
  <author>
    <autor />
  </author>
  <authority>
    <autority />
  </authority>
  </aFile>
 </syntax>
```

Fig.9. Partial code of syntax thesaurus

```
<?xml version="1.0" ?>
- <synonym from="resource generator">
  - <event orginal="incidence rate">
      <seeAlso>incidence proportion</seeAlso>
      <seeAlso>rate of incidence</seeAlso>
      <seeAlso>proportion of incidence</seeAlso>
    </event>
  - <period orginal="2010-2012">
      <seeAlso>2010 to 2012</seeAlso>
      <seeAlso>20010</seeAlso>
      <seeAlso>2011</seeAlso>
      <seeAlso>2012</seeAlso>
    </period>
  - <location orignal="northern great plains">
      <seeAlso>northern plains</seeAlso>
    </location>
  </synonym>
```

Fig.10. Partial code of synonym thesaurus

Implementation of Resource Storage (RS) Component

In the RS component, the method displayResource() identifies resource types by parsing RDF and gets resources for users. RDF is easily parsed using PHP. Because RDF is an XML based file, many XML query techniques such as XPath, Simple XML, XML DOM and so forth that can be used to read and write data to RDF. In the implementation of ISSS, XPath is used for parsing RDF. Fig.11 shows the partial code of the RS component.

```
class ResourceStorage
{ function displayResource($theme, $event, $location,
     $period, $style)
 {//check resource type
   checkResourceType ($style);
   //get resource from the resource storage
   fetchResource($theme, $event, $location, $period, $style);
 }
 function   fetchResource($theme,   $event,   $location,$period,
$style)
  { ...
    $xmlRDF = new DOMDocument();
    $xmlRDF -> load(RDF);
    $xmlRDFXpath = new DOMXPath($xmlRDF);
    $resource = $xmlRDFXPath->
  query("//theme[@id='".$theme."']/
  event[@id='".$event."']/location[@id='".$location."']/
  period[@id='".$period."']/style[@id='".$style."']");
   ...
  }
}
```

Fig.11. Partial code of RS component

Implementation of Search Engine (SE) Component

In SE component, the operation *searchProperties()* parses the inference rule file and infers resource properties via the extracted information or user's indication. After all the needed properties are inferred and collected by SM, it communicates with RS to get the target resource. Fig. 12 shows the partial code of the function searchProperty.

```
class SearchEngine
{ ...
  //search the properties of target resource
  function searchProperty()
  { searchTheme();       searchEvent();       searchLocation();
    searchPeriod();      searchStyle();
  }
}
```

Fig. 12. Partial code of SE component

Implementation of Resource Generation (RG) Component

RG provides a user interface in resource generator's view to let resource generators indicate all the information for each resource property when they are creating resources. The operation *addForResource()* takes resource properties' information and communicates with RS to write the information into RDF. *addForSourceCheck()* opens and parses the Inference Rule file to add the resource information into the file. RG collects synonym information of resource properties from the resource generator, and *addForThesaurus()* adds synonyms into the Synonym Thesaurus. Fig. 13 shows the partial code of the implementation of the RG component.

```
class GenerateResource
{ ...
 //function to add resource to RDF
 function addResource($staticmapfiles, $name, $theme,
   $event, $location, $period)
 {...}
 //add resource to inference
 function addForResourceCheck($staticmapfiles, $theme,
    $event, $location, $period)
 { ... }
 //add resource to thesaurus
 function addForThesaurus($theme, $event, $location,
      $period, $synonym1, $synonym2, $synonym3)
 {...}
}
```

Fig. 13. Partial code of RG component

Implementation of ISSS Plug-In

ISSS plug-in class is implemented to address objective 3 for providing reusability. The independent module ISSS plug-in can be instantiated for plugging ISSS into any existed web site for image retrieving. The plug-in class provides operations for configuring both the source file and the destination file, and then it ships ISSS to the plugged site. Partial code of the ISSS Plug-In is shown in Fig. 14.

```
class ISSS
{ protected $newPath;     protected $sourcePath;
  protected $jsPath;      protected $cssPath;
  protected $pluginFile;  protected $componentName;
  public function ISSSPlugIn()
  { //config ISSS component
     $this->configApplication();
     //setup ISSS component
    $this->setupModules($this->newPath, $this->sourcePath);
   //plug ISSS component
   $this->PagePlugIn();
  }
 public function configApplication()
 {   // code for setting up the $componentName, $newPath,
     //$sourcePath, $jsPath, $cssPath, pluginFile
 }
 public function shipFiles($newAppPath, $fwaPath)
 { // code for shipping the needed files to the destination  }
 public function PagePlugIn()
 { // code for plug the search page to the website }
}
```

Fig. 14. Partial code of ISSS plug-in

6 Use of ISSS

6.1 Plug In ISSS

The design and implementation of ISSS supports reusability. It can be plugged into any website as an image retrieval system. To plug ISSS in, the developer needs to (1) configure and setup ISSS by indicating both the ISSS source file path and target path; and (2) plug- ISSS user interface into any web page by indicating the path of that page. The following shows an example of plugging ISSS to an existing website EASTWeb[11]. EASTWeb is a collaborative project involving scientists from South Dakota State University and the USGS Center for Earth Resources Observation and Science (EROS), along with partners from government agencies, and nongovernmental organizations. EASTWeb collects various types of images of public health maps, and it provides public access to the web users to retrieve these image resources. ISSS is plugged into EASTWeb to facilitate web users to retrieve web resources.

i. Indicate all the paths for plugging ISSS into EASTWeb

```
$newPath="eastweb/ISSS";
$sourcePath="web/ISSS";
$jsPath="web/js";
$cssPath="web/css";
$pluginFile="eastweb/homepage.html";
$componentName="eastweb/search";
```

ii. Instantiating the new ISSS

```
$eastwebISSS=new ISSS();
```

iii. Invoking the plug-in method

```
$eastwebISSS->ISSSPlugIn($newPath, $sourcePath,
    $jsPath, $cssPath, $pluginFile, $componentName);
```

After the setup and plug-in of ISSS is complete, the search interface is displayed in the plugged page. EASTWeb ISSS is ready to be used by the end users to search image resource.

6.2 Resource Seeker's View

ISSS provides a search text box to users for typing target resource information and a button to start searching resources. Fig.15 displays the EASTWeb searching UI.

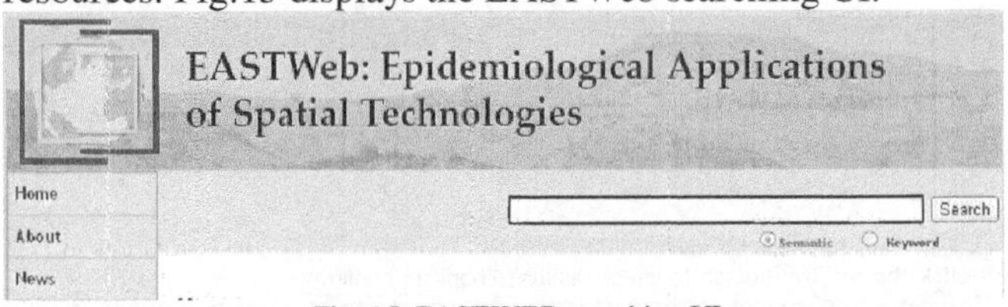

Fig. 15. EASTWEB searching UI

After a user types the content for describing the target resource, ISSS will extract the information and try to get the result by inferring each property of the resource. ISSS provides resource seekers user friendly interfaces with recommended resource properties for indicating "unknown" properties. Fig. 16-19 shows the searching processes of property indication. In the example, the resource information "wnv hot spot kml" is typed in the text box by users. "wnv" is extracted by ISSS to be the theme of the resource, "hot spot" and "kml" are treated as the resource's event and style. For the unknown information, it provides the recommended options of location and period to users.

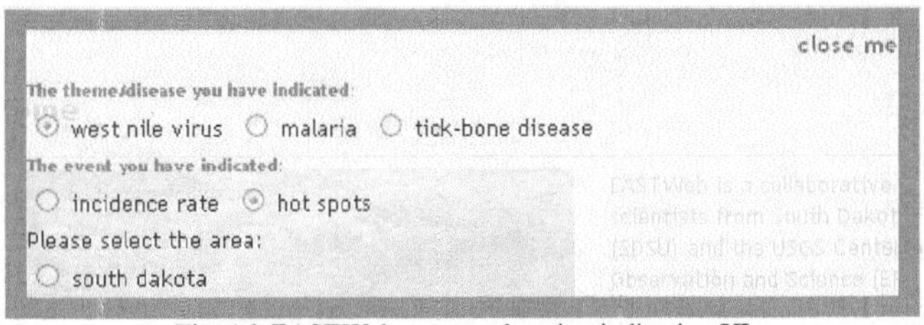

Fig. 16. EASTWeb resource location indicating UI

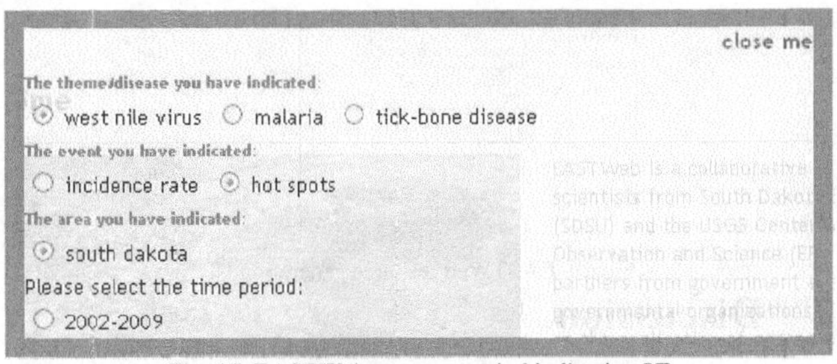

Fig. 17. EASTWeb resource period indicating UI

6.3 Resource Generator's View

ISSS provides user interfaces for generating resource in resource generator's view. Resource generators can create resources by giving all the information of the resource. As soon as the resource is created by the generator, it is stored in Resource Storage. Fig.20 shows the resource generation interface. It is the generator's responsibility to provide the information of *theme*, *event*, *location*, *period*, and *style*. When an image is being uploaded, its *style* property can be automatically extracted by the system from its type extension. The generator can also illustrate the synonyms that will the used in the Synonym Thesaurus for semantics interpretation.

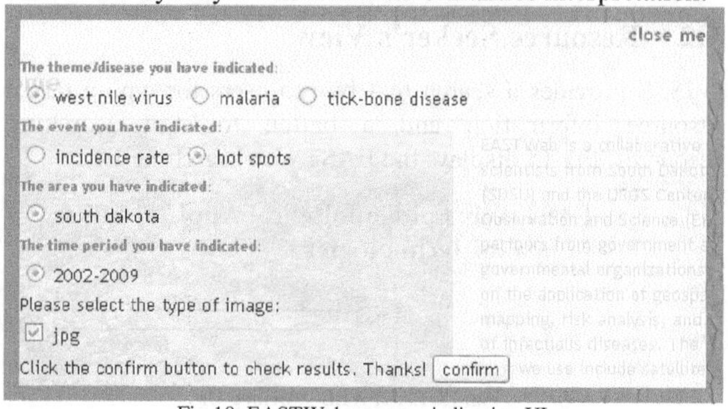

Fig.18. EASTWeb resource indicating UI

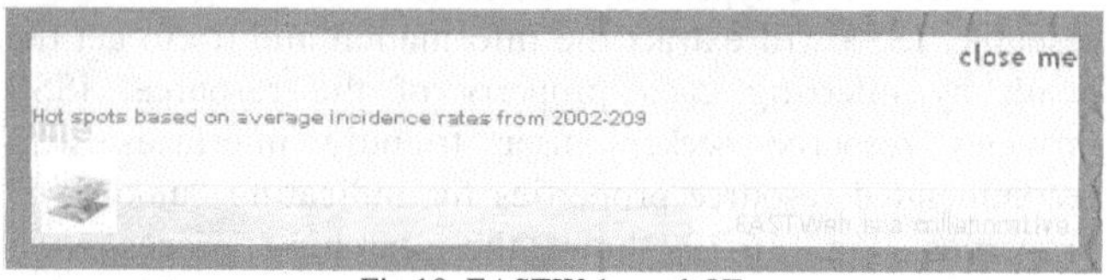

Fig.19. EASTWeb result UI

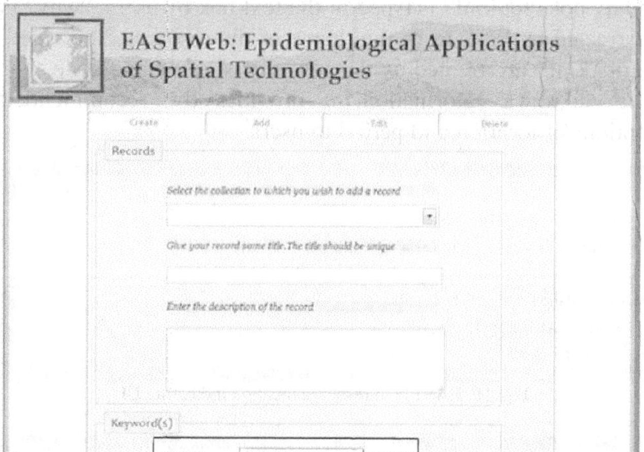

Fig.20. EASTWeb resource generation UI

7 Discussion

ISSS is designed and developed for searching and retrieving web image resources and it facilitates the construction of web based image search system websites. ISSS is designed with the aim for user friendliness, relevant search results and reusability of implementation. In order to address the user friendliness and result relevancy, we adopted the sematic web approach and designed a methodology for describing resources, extracting information, organizing resource properties and inferring resources to interpret both users and resources for retrieving target resources thoroughly. The architectural design of the system addressed the reusability.

Section 6 uses a case study to presents the reusability of the ISSS system. The achievement of the user-friendliness and result relevancy is evaluated based on the results from a focus group survey. Two Focus Groups with eight members in each participated in a survey containing questionnaires addressing the user friendly interfaces and search result relevancy. The first group was given a 35-minute presentation on ISSS and the second group was given a 5-minute instruction on how to use the semantic search function in a testing website. None of the participants has experience in developing a semantic search engine. A specific task was given to the participants for conducting a search. 94% of the participants think that ISSS is user friendly and the user interface is meaningful and straightforward to use. 100% of participants agree with that ISSS always provides relevant results without any duplicated or useless accompany. Based on these results, we believe ISSS successfully achieved the objectives of user friendly interface and result relevancy.

It can be concluded that ISSS is an image retrieving system, which is user- friendly, result relevant, and reusable.

8 Acknowledgment

This work is supported by NIH grant R01AI079411 "*An Integrated System for the Epidemiological Application of Earth Observation Technologies*".

9 References

[1] W3C Semantic Web Activity. http://www.w3.org/2001/sw/.

[2] T. Berners-Lee. "Weaving the Web". Harper, San Francisco, CA, 1999.

[3] D. Fensel, Wahlster, W., Lieberman, H., Hendler, J., eds.: "Spinning the Semantic Web: Bringing the World Wide Web to Its Full Potential". MIT Press, 2002.

[4] G. Jane. "Dublin Core: History, Key Concepts, and Evolving Context". DC-2010 International Conference on Dublin Core and Metadata Applications. October 20, 2010.

[5] P. Steve. "Expressing Dublin Core in Topic Maps". Lecture notes in Computer Science volume 4999, pp. 186-197. 2008.

[6] Dublin Core Metadata Initiative website. http://dublincore.org/documents/dces/.

[7] SPARQL. http://en.wikipedia.org/wiki/SPARQL.

[8] PHP: Hypertext Preprocessor. http://us.php.net/.

[9] J.J Garrett. "Ajax: A New Approach to Web Applications". http://www.adaptivepath.com/ideas/essays/archives/000385.php.

[10] Cascading Style Sheets. http://www.w3.org/Style/CSS/Overview.en.html.

[11] EASTWeb project. http://globalmonitoring.sdstate.edu/projects/eastweb/.

SESSION

ONTOLOGIES

Chair(s)

TBA

Personal Ontology–based Sentiment Analysis System for Mobile Devices

Sang-Min Park[1], Doo-Kwon Baik[1]
[1]Dept. of Computer and Radio Communications Engineering, Korea University, Seoul, Republic of Korea
wiyard@korea.ac.kr, baikdk@korea.ac.kr

Abstract—*The increasing proliferation of mobile devices has resulted in people being able to express their opinions and sentiments more easily. To obtain people's preferences and evaluations about products and services, sentiments expressed over Websites and social network services need to be analyzed. However, due to the diversity of the media and the short lengths of messages, the sentiment data is fragmented and distributed. Nowadays, products are equipped with numerous functions, so product features are diverse and complex. In order to solve the sentiment data fragmentation problem and the complexity of the feature, we propose an ontology-based sentiment analysis system for mobile devices.*

Keywords: Ontology, Sentiment analysis, Mobile device

1 Introduction

Social network services such as Facebook and Twitter and blogs have expanded due to the proliferation of mobile devices. Personal opinions about products can be easily posted and shared over the Web and on social networks, and people can easily obtain other people's opinion by conducting Web and social network searches. With these data, there is no need to enter each item individually. However, this data is unstructured; this type of data has also been described as fragmentary because of the constraints of microblogging. Because reviews are scattered, it is difficult to obtain a comprehensive understanding of the overall opinion of everyone. An overall analysis of the review data created by professional power bloggers is hard to find as the data are subdivided according to each feature. In order to solve these problems, decision making by collecting and analyzing the opinions on the Web and on social networks is carried out. The methods used are called sentiment analysis methods.

Sentiment analysis can be divided into document-level, sentence-level, word-level, and feature-level analyses. Document-level analysis determines the polarity of the document according to the frequency and location of a specified term. Sentence-based analysis focuses on sentence-level adjectives. Word-based polarity analysis makes word lists that have polarity and extends them with WordNet. Finally, feature-based sentiment analysis finds frequent nouns and noun phrases in order to extract frequent features; it analyzes sentiments for these extracted features [1].

Initial studies considered preferences with respect to the overall target product itself. However, people's opinions and sentiments are complex. Thus, it was found that detailed classification and evaluation were needed of the features of the products. However, the problem is that detailed information on the features is inadequate for learning with a reasonable dataset. As an alternative, structured data can be used to obtain such knowledge by leveraging domain ontology [2]. It can conjugate the ontology mapping because ontologies have structural information that facilitates such an activity. Ontology structure can embody the kind of feature using a hierarchical domain with less data. By means of these ontology-based sentiment analyses, users can collect public opinions and preferences in detail for a feature.

Three aspects of these sentiment analysis methods make them suitable for mobile device environments. First, data generated on mobile devices can be personally gathered and in various forms of information than on a PC for public use. Fragmented data can be integrated into one role based on the user. Second, sentiments containing personal information need to be kept private. It is more suitable to keep personal information on a mobile device than on the Web. Private information has to be handled inside a mobile device to minimize access by external processes. Third, to analyze a user in the new media, a certain amount of data is needed. These cold start problems can be resolved by utilizing unused existing data pertaining to users on mobile devices.

Nowadays, products include various functions, resulting in diverse and complex features. Because previous approaches simply constructed feature lists from public opinions, a separate process is needed to evaluate the products according to their own priorities [3]. Domain-specific fine-grained features can be difficult for users to understand because the term itself may be strange to understand. There are differences depending on the level of the individual and the public's preferred level. Positive rating details vary with the characteristics of the public, and even the results may vary with personal preference. In order to solve these two problems, a system that reflects personal standards and that supports a hierarchical architecture is required for understanding fine-grained features easily.

In this paper, we propose a personal sentiment analysis system for mobile phones using feature-level ontology. Our proposed system analyzes the differences between personal preferences and the public's preferences. The former is extracted from mobile phones, whereas the latter is extracted from the Web and social networks. Personal preference is determined by the weights of different features and is provided to readers as a reference when a user writes a review. The system is configured on camera lens domain. We chose one product for feasibility tests and applied the results obtained to other products to determine whether the selected feature is appropriate.

2 Related Work

The uses of ontology-based text mining can be divided into four kinds: utilization of text classification in ontology evaluation, use of a domain-specific ontology in mapping, enhancement of the results of text classification, and use of domain ontology for classification. In particular, ontology-based sentiment analysis has been used for feature recognition using domain ontology to reduce the number of sentiment analyses [4] and secondary data mining techniques to reduce the number of rules in the rule-based classification [5]. There are dictionaries, such as SentiWordNet, that calculate polarity. Using these dictionaries, the polarity of each term can be obtained [6]. Sentiment Ontology Tree (SOT) study for product reviews includes the adding of sentiment value to the ontology-based feature tree [7]. Recently, it has been found that fragmentary comments of about 140 characters in social media such as Twitter need an efficient technique to extract meaningful sentiment information. In recent years, some studies have been conducted to extract sentiment in mobile devices because of the prevalence of smartphones. However, those analyses were limited to one media like SMS and Twitter [8].

3 Proposed System

Content-based analysis methods that use previous purchases and collaborative filtering analysis using the data of neighbors with similar inclinations can be used to generate recommendations. A general analytical model deals with one medium only. However, accurate analysis is difficult because of the fragmentary nature of microblogs. Our proposed model conducts analyses using data on the previous representation of individuals in a variety of media stored on smartphones. Personal opinion is expressed in various ways, but can be collected from a variety of media and mobile devices. Thus, this proposed system can integrate continuous information and opinions about one topic. The system comprises a Collective Sentiment Ontology Tree (CSOT) configuration module, data storage modules, a Personal Sentiment Ontology Tree (PSOT) configuration module, and an individual character extraction module. These modules are described below:

- CSOT configuration module: The system uses data about a specific topic, from social media such as Twitter Search and Web page history. In the preprocessing step, Tokenization, POS Tagging, and NER are carried out on the information gathered. The module extracts features using domain ontology and constructs an ontology tree based on the extracted features. It also uses SentiWordNet to calculate the polarity of the sentence that contains the feature, and makes instances of the CSOT ontology tree that include weighted polarity of terms.

- Data storage modules: These data modules are separated according to the three characteristics of the storage media of a mobile device. There is an internal saving module (which deals with messages, kakaotalk, history, etc.), an external saving module (which deals with information from Facebook, Twitter, Webpages, etc.), and a streaming module (which deals with calls, TV data, streaming information, etc.). Because the internal saving module uses local data storage, it easily handles the information. The external saving module is based on requests using parameters such as keywords; it stores the response data from servers. The streaming module cannot store all of the streaming data; therefore, it stores sentiment with features using SOT.

- PSOT configuration module: Either one big SOT or one SOT for each application can be stored. Because some applications can be removed, individual SOT structures are better to maintain. This technique also has an advantage over CSOT when using the same media. When a target topic has been determined, it merges all the individual SOTs constructed by each application into one SOT. It can also be extended using an external domain ontology, in which case the SOT can obtain more domain information and have a more hierarchical structure. The preprocessing step is also responsible for Tokenization and POS Tagging, and NER on the information gathered. However, it uses a feature-based ontology tree created previously in the CSOT configuration module because the amount of personal data is relatively small.

- Individual character extraction module: Personal polarity can be measured by comparing PSOT with CSOT. One is the personal information generated by internal applications such as browser bookmarks,

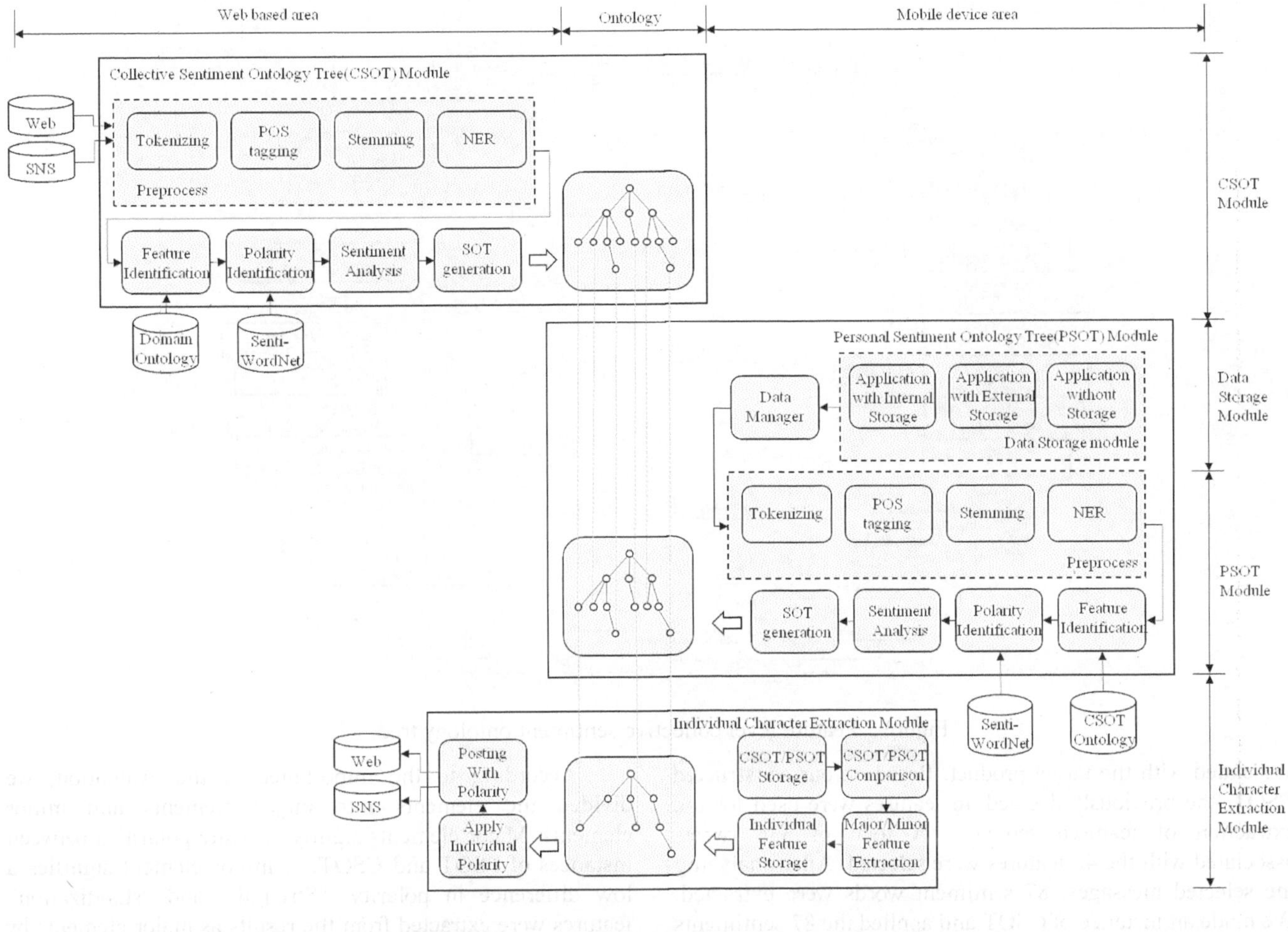

Figure 1 The architecture of personal ontology-based sentiment analysis system

messenger, and SMS on mobile devices. The other is public information located on the Web and in social network data. It divides the data into major factors and minor factors depending on the degree of deviation by comparing the instance polarity value of CSOT and PSOT about the extracted features. The deviation in personal and public sentiment analysis of the target product is considered per individual character. Thus, it is easy to take advantage of the new product because it uses already existing data on mobile device.

Users can know their own feature preferences and sentiments by personal polarity. Instead of the ambiguous recommendation for a product, users can check the interest or dislike feature ratings. Thus, recommendations can be made that reflect the characteristics of individuals based on analysis of the existing information. A hierarchical ontology can identify the feature preferences with less personal data using the higher-level feature preferences. Locally stored ontology on mobile devices can be reused in a similar domain, without compromising privacy because the operation is done internally. When people write reviews that include their personal polarity, they can be helpful to other people. Instead of sharing a simple expression such as "like," a review can provide additional information about the writer. The information gathered is "what kind of people like it."

4 Use case

In order to demonstrate the feasibility of our proposed system, we chose camera lenses as the target domain. The major features of the lenses are different and depend on the purpose of usage; in addition, optical-related features are difficult to understand. There are various emotional preferences and expressions associated with pictures.

For our experiments, we chose Canon EF 200 mm USM lens as our target product and used the personal data of people who are interested in these products. We found 447 sentences containing the name of the target product on 20,354 history pages. The sentiment word was contained in 139 sentences among 447 sentences. From those sentences, 46 features were extracted. Using the 46 features, CSOT was constructed. We applied 139 sentiments on the instance of history CSOT. Using Daum twitter search (http://www.daum.net), we searched 139,000 tweets

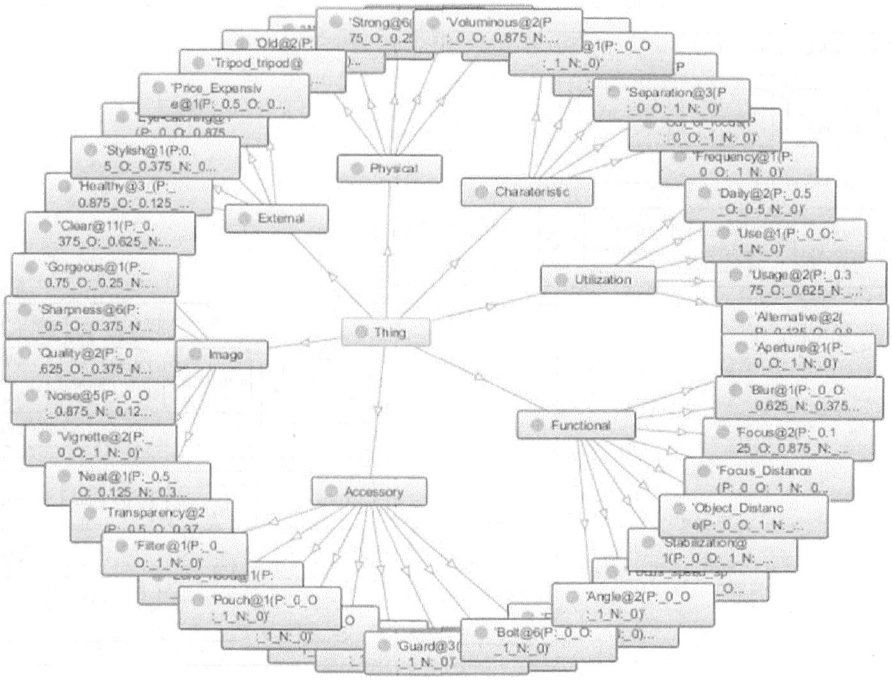

Figure 2 Feature level collective sentiment ontology tree

associated with the target product. Based on our constructed CSOT, the previously decided 46 features were used for the extraction of featured sentence. A total of 336 tweets associated with the 46 features were selected. After analyzing the selected messages, 87 sentiment words were extracted. We made an instance of CSOT and applied the 87 sentiments on the instance of Twitter CSOT.

In the mobile device environment, we extracted 132 personal datasets associated with the target camera lenses from Twitter (http://www.twitter.com), SMS, bookmark, Facebook (http://www.facebook.com), kakaotalk (messenger application; http://www.kakao.com/talk), tistory (blog; http://www.tistory.com), and slrclub (DSLR review site; http://www.slrclub.com). There were 21 sentiment sentences. Those sentiment sentences included 17 features. Based on the 17 features, a PSOT was constructed and the 21 sentiments applied on the instance of PSOT.

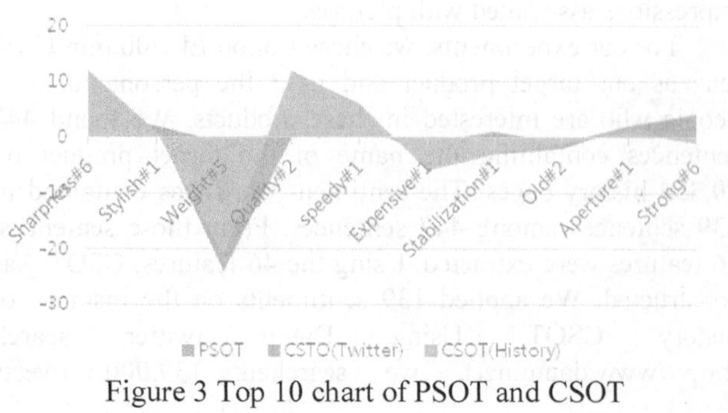

Figure 3 Top 10 chart of PSOT and CSOT

According to the importance of the evaluation, we divided the elements into major elements and minor elements. Major elements signify opposite polarities between instances of PSOT and CSOT. A minor element signifies a low difference in polarity. "Strength" and "stabilization" features were extracted from the results as major elements by comparing the value of the polarity between PSOT and history CSOT. The "stylish" feature was extracted as a minor factor between PSOT and history CSOT.

In the Twitter CSOT and PSOT case, "Image stabilization" had a different polarity value, so it was extracted as a major element. From these comparisons of PSOT, history CSOT, and Twitter CSOT, "Strength" and "Image stabilization" were regarded as major elements and "Stylish" as a minor element of the personal weighted feature. When we constructed PSOT, history CSOT, and Twitter CSOT about Canon EF 24 mm and 85 mm USM lens in the same way, there was no conflict between them and the previously extracted major and minor elements.

5 Conclusions

In this study, a personal sentiment ontology tree was constructed using data extracted from individual applications on a mobile device according to temporal relevance. PSOT, constructed from data on a mobile device, was compared with CSOT constructed from data on the Web and social networks. A personalized sentiment feature was extracted between them. Our proposed system was able to extract major and minor elements of personal features in a feasibility test conducted using camera lenses. Personalized polarity is a factor that can increase the accuracy of recommendation systems. The polarity information of a writer can help other people to consider his reviews. In order to demonstrate the performance of the system, we are currently developing an automated system for large-scale testing, and we plan to analyze the temporal relevance of topics in each media.

6 Acknowledgement

The corresponding author is Doo-Kwon Baik.

7 References

[1] ABDELMONEIM, DAREEN MAMDOUH SALAMA. “Semantic deontic modeling and text classification for supporting automated environmental compliance checking in construction”. Diss. University of Illinois, 2011.

[2] Lili Zhao and Chunping Li. "Ontology based opinion mining for movie reviews". Knowledge Science, Engineering and Management, Springer Berlin Heidelberg, 204-214, 2009.

[3] Manolis Maragoudakis , Euripidis Loukis, and Yannis Charalabidis. "A Review of Opinion Mining Methods for Analyzing Citizens' Contributions in Public Policy Debate". Electronic Participation. Springer Berlin Heidelberg, 298-313, 2011.

[4] Khin Phyu Phyu Shein, Thi Thi Soe Nyunt. "Sentiment classification based on Ontology and SVM Classifier". Communication Software and Networks, 2010. ICCSN'10. Second International Conference on, IEEE, 2010.

[5] Nandhini, M., M. Janani, S. N. Sivanandham. "Association rule mining using swarm intelligence and domain ontology". Recent Trends In Information Technology (ICRTIT), 2012 International Conference on. IEEE, 2012.

[6] Baccianella, Stefano, Andrea Esuli, and Fabrizio Sebastiani. "Sentiwordnet 3.0: An enhanced lexical resource for sentiment analysis and opinion mining". Proceedings of the 7th conference on International Language Resources and Evaluation (LREC'10), Valletta, Malta, May 2010.

[7] Wei, Wei, and Jon Atle Gulla. "Sentiment learning on product reviews via sentiment ontology tree". Proceedings of the 48th Annual Meeting of the Association for Computational Linguistics, Association for Computational Linguistics, 2010.

[8] Chambers, Lorraine, et al. "Mobile sentiment analysis". 2012.

University Ontology: case study Ahlia University

K. Hadjar[1] and N. Chanane[1]
[1]Department of Multimedia, Ahlia University, Al Manama, Bahrain

Abstract - *The huge amount of information available on the internet (and intranets) and its unstructured nature is reaching a point that some actions has to be taken in order to ease the use of queries within a web search engine. The introduction of order/organization and structure is necessary for the process of this information. One-step toward this goal is the use of ontologies for specific areas/domains. The word ontology is becoming widespread and its use in organizing the web is gaining momentum. Many scientists are working on semantic webs, which are considered as intelligent and meaningful webs. The lack of university ontology made me develop such one. A case study was developed to validate my ontology: Ahlia University, Bahrain.*

Keywords: Ontology, Abstract Model, University.

1. Introduction

Nowadays the web has shifted into another dimension: the semantics. The language of the web: HTML has embraced semantics into its last version: version 5. Almost all the fields have their own ontology. Since I am in the field of academics since a while, and I have noticed that there is few serious development of university ontology, I have decided to build one.
Several tools and methods have been developed to build ontologies. Rather than focusing all the attention to information, it was all in the core concepts in using ontology and its relationships. The most well-known and widespread tool for editing and developing ontologies is Protégé [10]. Its Graphical User Interface (GUI) lets the developers concentrate on the concept rather than thinking about the syntax of the output language. Protégé has pliable data design and extendible plug-ins. In this paper, definition of the University concept is clarified through the university ontology. Creating a university ontology using Protégé is the object of this paper. Ahlia University is taken as a case study for the development of the ontology and several phases are outlined e.g., superclass, hierarchy of subclasses, creating subclasses instances, retrieving queries, graphs and visualization views. The case study is limited to few departments and courses, as an example. This implies that since the model works for one university, it will work for other universities, with minor changes.
This paper is organized as follows: in section 2 I discuss the steps required for building the university ontology. Section 3 presents my case study: "Ahlia University". In section 4, some queries applied on the Ahlia University ontology are exposed. Finally section 5 concludes this paper.

2. University Ontology

There is many data shared between organizations and organization divisions, which can be used in building up the university structure. Yet there did not seem to be a suitable shared terminology for presenting such information in linked data. Based on the need of a clear structure for any organization, I have developed university ontology as the basic structure model to share between all organizations who do not like to start from scratch.
In fact a lightweight, highly reusable ontology, which did not try to model particular organizational structures, is required.

2.1 Building the ontology

To increase the ontology efficiency, I need to ensure that Ontology is defined as a formal specification, explicit and consensual conceptualization of a domain [5]. Definitely, the development and design of Ontology supports people to recognize and answer the doubts of domains [1]. It comprises of a group of concepts related together in an organizational method. In this paper, I focus on specialized Ontology that is domain ontology and task ontology. These are reusable Ontologies within a given domain, but not from one domain to another. While all tasks performed in a given domain are within the ontology [5]. According to Mizoguchi, Vanwelkenhuysen and Ikeda [6], the ontology task is to describe a curtain vocabulary related to a task. The reuse of ontology is critical. I have to build manually the ontology from scratch by following a known methodology.

2.2 Ontology Development Methodology

To ensure the consistency of ontology structure and increasing its efficiency, during development I have followed the guidelines from many sources. First, I have studied how to build ontology by using a guideline from [7]. The guide built using Protégé ontology editor [6], which is the same tool that we have used for the University Ontology development. I have studied a few ontology development methodologies and finally I have decided to follow a recently defined methodology from [4], incorporating with the guide from [5]. This ontology development covers the steps from the initiation phase to the data retrieval phase of ontology. Specification and Conceptualization are the two main steps available in this methodology. Obtaining knowledge about the domain is the objective of the first step. Moreover, organizing, structuring the information using exterior demonstrations independently from the environment and implementation language is the second objective.

2.2.1 *Specification*

The scope puts boundaries for the ontology; requiring what has to be involved and what has not. This step was suggested for an advance stage in the Ontology Development: A guide to creating your first ontology [5], is included at this stage to minimize the process of analyzing concepts and data, particularly for the range and difficulty of the University Model Ontology. The iterations for following verification, process will be adjusted when needed. I have considered the needs for elaborating the University structure project with theories related to higher education organizations. It is a first prototype and the considered concepts are not related to all divisions in an organization. Therefore, it includes general concepts for the university abstract model.

Previous domain analysis was necessary to be done as the first step. In this work, the presentation for framing the university structure and the relevant documents were collected from a number of organization charts of different universities. Furthermore, advices from management leaders of universities and faculty were put into consideration. Gruninger and Fox Methodology point of view [11] was taken into account. Problems arise when people need information but the systems don't provide it. The motivation scenarios are followed. In addition, templates have been used in order to define motivation scenarios and link them to the people involved. A set of solutions to all problems is made available whenever the semantic features can be resolved.

2.2.2 Conceptualization

In this step, the terms used in representing the most important entities in the university structure are enumerated as classes shown in Table 1. Definitions of the main classes are listed after the table. All the concepts appearing in the figure mostly focus on the main departments in any University e.g., AcademicAffairs, AdministrativeAffairs, President, Deans, Chairs, Faculty, Student, Courses, Library, Gym, WebSite, BookStore, etc…

Table 1. Key Item List as Class and Subclass

Class	Subclass
Courses	GraduateCourses
	UnderGraduateCourses
Programs	BachelorProgram
	MasterProgram
	PhDProgram
Person	Employee
	Students

- The class "Courses" is defined as the basic two categories of the courses available at most universities, "GraduateCourses" and "UnderGraduateCourses".
- The class "Programs", defined as the possible offered programs by universities at their start or at later stages of their program. And the three subclasses are, "BachelorProgram", "MasterProgram", and "PhDProgram".
- The class "Person" divides the people at the university to two types, Employees; staff and faculty, and Students.

The main relations, attributes and properties have been created as shown in Table 2.

Table 2. Relation between the University Model Classes

Class Name	Relation	Class Name	Inverse Relation
Department	hasHead	Chair	isHeadOf
Students	take	Courses	areTakenBy
Faculty	publishes	Articles	isPublishedBy
Classes	attendedBy	Students	attends

Figure 1, contains the object properties according to the relationship, which we want to add between the classes "Professor" "advises", and the courses "areOfferedBy".

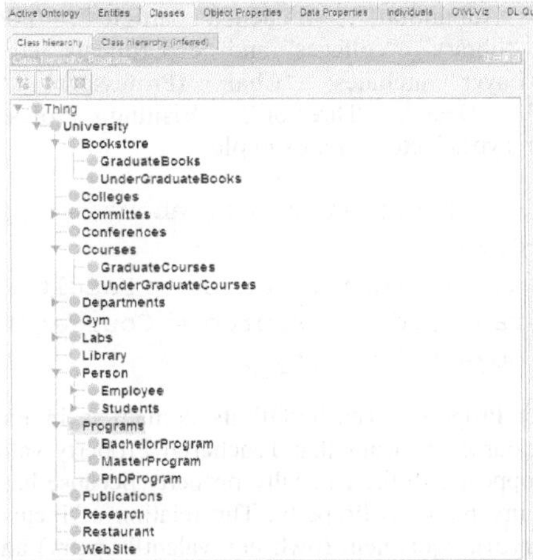

Figure 1. University Ontology Classes Hierarchy.

Table 3, illustrates the relationship between individual to data literal, for example the Course has "CRN ", "courseName ", "creditHours ".

Table 3. University Ontology ObjectProperty

Class	Property
Faculty	emailAddress
	mobile
Course	CRN
	courseName
	creditHours

In a general usage, a restriction can be a general form of instructions that sets a limited border defined for a function or a type of process. These relations were captured in a semantic diagram to represent the relations between components.

- Property and Relationship

Since having only classes cannot answer all the enquiries; defining links inside or between the classes is needed (such as properties). I have used property, which shows relationship between individual and individual, Relationships between Individuals at University Ontology Such as property, faculty as advisor of student. I have also defined Object Properties Domain & Ranges, for example:

```
<owl: Object Property rdf: about = advisor>
<rdfs: domain rdf: resource=student/>
<rdfs: range rdf: resource=faculty/>
</owl: object Property>
```

The Top layer of the university ontology there is: "Person", "course", "committee", "AcademicAfairs", "Admission", "University" etc... In the Middle layer of the university ontology there is: "AdminStaff", "Student", "articles", "books" and "subject", "library", "colleges" and "departments" etc. And the Bottom Layer includes: "Chair (Professor)", "Teaching Assistant", "Dean", "Director", "Visiting Professor" and "Professor Types", etc..., for example

```
<owl: object property rdf: about =
TeacherOf/>
<rdfs: domain rdf: resource = Faculty/>
<rdfs: range rdf: resource = Course />
</owl: object Property>.
```

The object Property –TeacherOf; its domain is in Faculty and range in Course. It means that TeacherOf Property value will be only just opposite to the isFaculty property because has Property is always inverse to is Property. The relation of Inclusion (rdfs: subPropetryof), equivalent (owl: equivalentPropetry) and Inverse (owl: inverseOf), and the limitation of function (owl:FunctionalPropetry) and inverse function (owl: InverseFunctionalProperty).

Since the conceptual model of the ontology has been created, the next step is to define related instances. For each instance, I have described: a name, the name of concept it belongs to, and its attribute values.

The instance (individual) is described first; then, the right class was selected, and finally its instances for the class are created.

Use rdf: type to state its class, and one instance can belong to many classes or many class belongs to same instances, for example;

```
</owl: thing rdf: about=
AdvancedDatabaseSystems >
<rdf: type rdf: resource= #course/>
<rdf: type rdf: resource= #student/>
</owl: thing>
```

Here it defines an individual or instance AdvancedDatabaseSystems, which belongs to the class "course and student. In which rdf: type has appeared twice, it shows that this instance belongs to two classes at the same time.

2.2.3 Implementation

I have chosen Protégé 4.1 in order to implement the ontology, due to its extensibility, quick prototyping and application development. Protégé ontologies are easily exported into different formats including RDF Schema, Web Ontology Language (OWL) and Top Braid Composer [9], which we have used at later stages in querying. Particularly, we have implemented the University Ontology in OWL. Structured relations are transformed into bidirectional relations while modeling in OWL. Moreover, only relations that are necessary in answering competence questions were modeled in ontology.

2.2.4 Verification

Consistency validation and classification are verified by using the Reasoner. During the process of charging classes and attributes, we used incremental and continuous verification to avoid future propagation errors. In the Reasoner, any class which is unsatisfiable is shown in red color indicating that error exists. At this point, it is very important to see how classes are defined (disjoint, isSubclassOf, Partial Class, Defined Class, etc...) and how are their restrictions (unionOf, allValuesFrom, etc...). Classification process is either for the whole ontology or for selected subtrees only. When the test is completed, the whole ontology, errors were listed, moving from bottom to upper level class. To compare the ontology execution with its conceptualization, graphs were generated using OWLViz [2] and OntoViz plug-ins [8].

3. Ahlia University Ontology

Ahlia University ontology defines elements to describe Ahlia University and its activities, which can occur between Departments, Faculty and Students. I have built the ontology based on the organization chart available on the University website and all data used for testing my work was also taken from the catalogue available. Since my base of the ontology was the university ontology, I only had to make some changes on the classes following the organization chart. Concepts (classes) such as, Departments, Degrees, Deans, Chairs, Faculty, Student, Courses, Library, CareerCenter, WebSite, ICTCenter, Labs ...etc, More relations (rules) where added between the Classes to show how they are related and linked to each other. The Ahlia University Ontology also includes relationships between classes. For instance, the relationship "teaches/isTaughtBy"is between Faculty class and Courses class. Other relationships are added, such as: hasHead/ isHeadOf, hadMember/isMemberOf, etc...

As shown in figure. 2, some of Ahlia University related classes and subclasses are listed. All the concepts appearing in the figure are mostly focused on the students, faculty and course based.

- The class "AhliaUniversity" is the highest-level class in this domain.
- The class "Assistant" defined as the basic two categories of the position of an Assistant available at most universities, ResearchAssistant and TeachingAssistant.
- The class "Professor", defined as the rank type of the faculty at the universities. I have listed its subclasses (AssistantProfessor, AssociateProfessor, FullProf and VisitingProf).

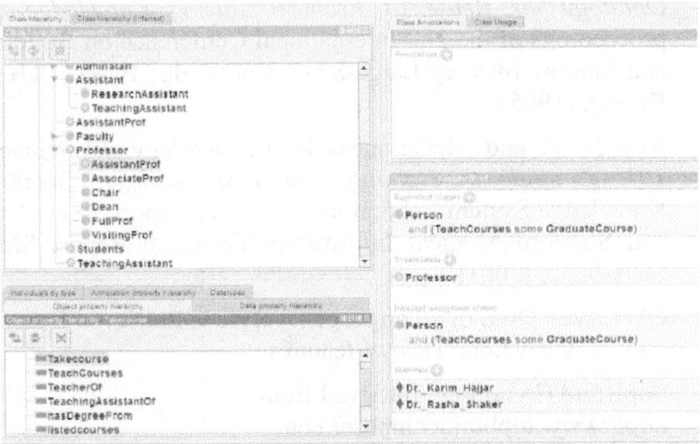

Figure 2. Ahlia University Ontology Class Hierarchy.

4. Query retrieval

A very powerful feature tab is available in Protégé, which is the DL Query. Considered as one of the basic plugins in Protégé 4 and is either available as a tab or a widget. It is based on the Manchester OWL syntax, which is a query language supported by the plugin, and a user-friendly syntax for OWL DL. A frame which fundamentally based on the information is collected about a specific class, individual or a property, into a single construct [7]. Here again, the query retrieval process has gone along the steps depicted in previous sections, and illustrated next figures (figure 3 and 4).

DL Query 1:

- Which courses does Dr. Karim teach?
- Courses_Offered and CourseFaculty value Dr_Al-Hadjar_Karim

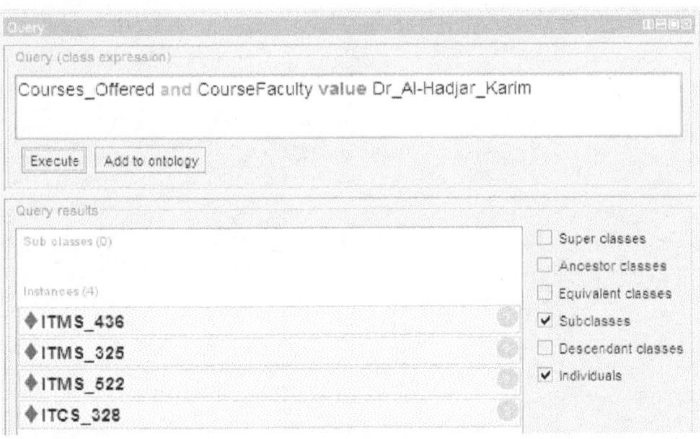

Figure. 3. Snapshot of the DL Query 1

DL Query 2:

- The list of available faculty on Saturday
- Course_Faculty and available value Saturday

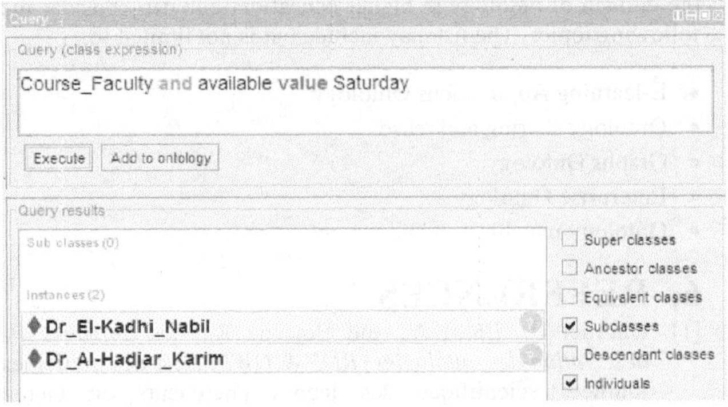

Figure. 4. Snapshot of the DL Query 2

Below, I have listed example of the data retrieved from the ontology using SPARQL query editor, available in TopBraid Composer.

Query :.

```
PREFIX rdf:<http://www.w3.org/1999/02/22-
rdf-syntax-ns#>
PREFIX uo:
<http://www.semanticweb.org/ontologies/2011/
9/Ontology1319571856122.owl#>
SELECT? X, ?Y, ?Z
WHERE
{?X rdf: type uo:Student
?Y rdf: type uo:Faculty
?Z rdf: type uo:Course
?X uo:advisor ?Y
?Y uo:teacherOf ?Z
?X uo:takesCourse ?Z }
```

Aside the features of Students class and hierarchy of Faculty class, most classes and properties used in this query can characterize it.

5. Conclusion

This paper presents my contribution to create University ontology. All the work done on Ahlia University Ontology was a reuse of the University Ontology that I have developed. Ahlia University Ontology describes all the departments under the University structure and the relationships that exist between them. I have modified the OWL version of the University Ontology and added more classes and restrictions based on the University organization chart of Ahlia University to get the final OWL of the Ontology. The ontology was expressed in OWL starting from creating classes and subclasses to properties, restrictions and instances. Then the owl file of the ontology is imported into TopBraid Composer for more powerful data retrieval software, to get the data needed from the ontology easily with short SPARQL queries. DL query in Protégé is also used for querying.

In ontologies, the focus is on relationships between concepts and not information itself. This work demonstrates the relations of university modules in the form of university ontology.

All the attention was given to the core concepts of using ontology and its relationships rather than information. As a future work in the domain of ontology in higher education, one can consider the following topics. The list may include but is not limited to,

- E-learning Applications Ontology
- Ontology sharing and reuse
- Graphs Ontology
- Enterprise Ontology
- Ontology matching and alignment

6. REFERENCES

[1] Ghorbel H., Bahri A., and Bouaziz R., *Les langages de description des ontologies: RDF & OWL*. Acte des huitièmes journées scientifique des jeunes chercheurs en Génie Electrique et Informatique (GEI), Sousse-Tunisia, (2008).

[2] Graphviz - Graph Visualization Software, Retrieved from http://www.graphviz.org

[3] Gruber T.R., A translation approach to portable ontology specifications, Knowledge Acquisition, 5 (2), pp 199-220, (1993).

[4] Gruninger M. and Fox M. S., *Methodology for the design and Evaluation of Ontologies*, IJCAI Workshop on Basic Ontological in Knowledge sharing, Montreal, Canada, (1995).

[5] Guarino N., *Formal Ontologies and information systems*. In proceedings of FOIS'98, IOS Press, Amsterdam, 1998.

[6] Mizoguchi R.,Vanwelkenhuysen J. and Ikeda M., *Task Ontology for Reuse of Problem Solving Knowledge*. In proceedings of the 2nd International Conference on Building and Sharing of Very Large-Scale Knowledge Bases. (KB & KS'95), (1995).

[7] Noy N. F. and McGuinness D. L. *Ontology development 101: A guide to creating your first ontology;* Stanford Knowledge System Laboratory Technical Report KSL-01-05 and Stanford Medical Informatics Technical Report SMI-2001-0880, (2001).

[8] OWL Web Ontology Language Overview, Retrieved from http://www.w3.org/TR/owl-features

[9] TopBraid Composer , retrieved from http://www.topbraidcomposer.com

[10] Protégé, Retrieved from http://protege.stanford.edu

[11] Zhao J., Wroe C., Goble., Stevens R., Quan D., and Greenwood M., *Using Semantic Web Technologies for Representing e-Science Provenance* in Proc 3rd International Semantic Web Conference ISWC2004, Hiroshima, Japan, Springer LNCS 3298, (2004).

Comparison Evaluation for SPARQL-to-SQL Translation Model

Hajung Sung[1], **Suckhoon Lee**[1], **and Doo-Kwon Baik**[1]
[1]Dept. of Computer Science and Radio Communications Engineering, Korea University, Seoul, Republic Of Korea
octoom@korea.ac.kr, leha82@korea.ac.kr, baikdk@korea.ac.kr

***Abstract** - Ontology use has increased with the increase in the use of the semantic Web. This has led to numerous research studies being conducted on ontology storage. SPARQL is a description language for the semantic Web environment and it searches ontology in an ontology database. However, it cannot search ontology in a relational database (RDB). To solve this problem, a data translation model and a query translation model have been proposed previously. However, these previous models have the disadvantage of requiring additional storage to store ontology. In this paper, we propose an SPARQL-to-SQL translation model that does not require additional ontology storage. The proposed model translates SPARQL into SQL to search data in an RDB. The data structure in such an RDB is a general data structure. As a result, the proposed model can search data stored in an RDB using SPARQL without requiring ontology storage. In addition, we describe models for comparison evaluation. The execution times of the models were evaluated in terms of five factors. The results of our evaluation showed that the proposed model is more efficient than other data translation models.*

Keywords: Ontology, Ontology Storage, SPARQL, SQL

1 Introduction

The use of ontology has increased with the increase in the use of the semantic Web. Much research [1-5] has been conducted on ontology storage for efficient ontology management. SPARQL, a query language for ontology recommended by W3C, can be used to search ontology in an ontology database. However, it cannot be used to search data stored in a relational database (RDB). For the expansion of the semantic Web, it is necessary to consider data stored in an RDB. Therefore, to solve this problem, a data translation model has been proposed. This model converts data stored in an RDB to ontology and then stores the ontology in an ontology database. However, this model suffers from the following limitation. This model requires additional storage, which leads to increased costs for converting data stored in an RDB to ontology. Therefore, to overcome this limitation of translation costs, query translation models have been proposed, a representative model being the SPARQL-to-SQL translation model [6-10]. However, these models require additional ontology storage. Therefore, a query translation model that does not require additional ontology storage needs to be developed.

In this paper, we propose an SPARQL-to-SQL translation model that does not require additional ontology storage. We further present models for comparison with our proposed model, and compare their performances in terms of SPARQL-to-SQL translation time, loading time of ontology storage, RDB-to-RDF translation time, query execution time, total translation time, and total runtime. We give a clear account of the comparison results to prove the efficiency of the proposed SPARQL-to-SQL translation model.

The rest of this paper is organized as follows. Section 2 gives an account of related work. Section 3 describes our proposed SPARQL-to-SQL translation model that does not require additional ontology storage. Section 4 presents models for comparison with our proposed model and the results of a quantitative evaluation. Finally, Section 5 gives concluding remarks.

2 Related Work

Currently, extensive research has been conducted on ontology storage based on RDB with SPARQL. These studies can be divided mainly based on SPARQL-to-SQL translation models and data translation models. Representative studies of data translation models include the Virtuoso, D2RQ, and RDBToOnto [11,12,13]. A data translation model converts data stored in an RDB to ontology, and then stores the ontology in an ontology database.

Virtuoso is a server-based system that supports Windows and Linux operating systems. It is an ontology database that is also designed to enable the integration and access of data in the form of XML and RDF. Virtuoso is built on the basis of a physical storage. It can search data in an ontology database using SPARQL. Virtuoso can be either commercial or non-commercial and it uses Jena and Sesame APIs through Jena and Sesame providers, respectively. In this paper, we conducted experiments on the noncommercial version of Virtuoso.

D2RQ converts data stored in an RDB into ontology using a mapping approach. The ontology is automatically generated by the system and stored in the memory. This generated ontology can be retrieved by using SPARQL.

RDBToOnto is a study in progress in the TAO project through which data stored in an RDB is converted into ontology. RDBToOnto describes the rich semantics of data stored in the RDB and supports automatic classification, which is performed using RTAXON learning methods. The relation of a word to its category is recognized as a subClassOf relationship according to the rules defined in RTAXON. In addition, the constraints defined by the user can be added, and a normalization function is provided to avoid duplication of data. Lastly, a convenient user interface is also provided. However, RDBToOnto only converts data stored in the RDB into ontology and then stores it as a file. Therefore, a model such as Fuseki can retrieve ontology using SPARQL. The above data translation model does not guarantee data consistency of ontology in the ontology database and the data stored in RDB. This problem is caused by the additional ontology storage. Changes in the data stored in the RDB and that stored in the ontology database cannot be changed simultaneously. In addition, data translation is time-consuming. Therefore, it is not suitable for processing large amounts of data.

3 Proposed SPARQL-to-SQL Model

Much research on SPARQL-to-SQL translation models has been conducted to overcome the disadvantages of data translation models. However, thus far, proposed SPARQL-to-SQL translation models support ontology storage based on RDB only. Therefore, this model needs additional ontology storage. In this paper, we propose an SPARQL-to-SQL translation model for general data in an RDB and compare the performance of the model with a data translation model.

Figure 1 illustrates the proposed model, which consists of the following four steps.

- Preprocessing: The SPARQL entered by the user is analyzed and converted into SQL for ontology storage based on RDB.

- RDB to Triple Mapping: The RDB components are mapped to RDF components in this step. The mapping information is stored in the form of OWL files should be prepared in advance by the user.

- SPARQL-to-SQL Translation: SQL statements obtained in the preprocessor step are converted into statements for querying data stored in an RDB referred by a mapping file. The RDB has a general schema.

- Search Results: Data stored in the RDB are retrieved and the query results are sent to the user.

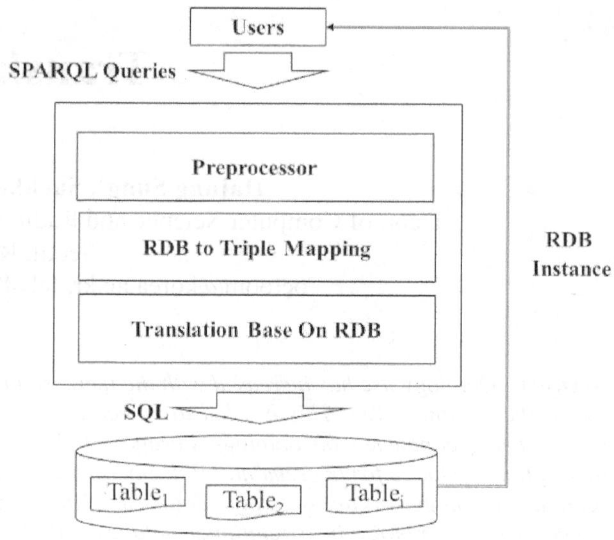

Figure 1 Proposed Model

4 Comparison Evaluation

In this section, we describe the preliminary constraints, factors, and notations relevant to the model for a comparison evaluation. In addition, we compare the performances of Virtuoso, Fuseki, D2RQ, and the proposed model.

4.1 Factors and Notation

The models to be compared are affected by the following five main factors:

- f1 : Number of RDB instances
- f2 : Loading time of ontology storage
- f3 : RDB-to-RDF translation time
- f4 : Query execution time
- f6 : SPARQL-to-SQL translation time
- f5 : Query pattern, which affect the translation time

Table 1 shows notations and their description.

Table1 Notations used in this study

Notations	Description
STT	SPARQL-to-SQL Translation Time
LT	Loading Time of ontology storage
RTT	RDB-to-RDF translation time
QET	Query execution time
TT	Total translation time
TRT	Total runtime

4.2 Models for comparison and evaluation

Figure 2 shows the models for comparison evaluation using SPARQL to query the data stored in the RDB. We determine the TRT of Virtuoso and Fuseki through the following two steps. In the first step, the RTT is obtained by RDBToOnto. Then, the LT, which is the time to load ontology to an ontology database, of these models can be obtained. Finally, we can obtain the TT, which is the sum of RTT and LT. D2RQ converts data stored in the RDB automatically into ontology and then loads it to an ontology database. Therefore, the TT of D2RQ is composed of only LT. Similarly, the TT of the SPARQL-to-SQL translation model is composed of only STT. For each model, the TRT is the sum of TT and QET. Therefore, TRT is the main factor for comparison evaluation. The next section shows the results for the TRT. The query languages used in the experiment were presented by the LUBM Q1, Q2, Q3, Q11, and Q14 [14]. The rest of the query was excluded because it did not fit in the search data stored in RDB.

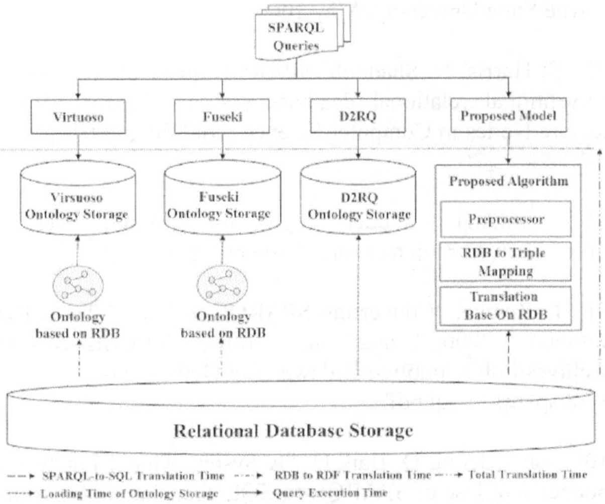

Figure 2 Models for comparison evaluation

4.3 Assumptions

For comparison evaluation, we made the following assumptions and considered various definitions:

- All data are stored in an RDB.
- The TRT is composed of QET and TT.
- The TT is composed of RTT and LT in Virtuoso and Fuseki.
- The TT is composed of LT in D2RQ.
- The TT is composed of STT in the SPARQL-to-SQL translation model.
- Virtuoso and Fuseki convert data stored in the RDB into ontology using a file created using RDBToOnto.
- Virtuoso and Fuseki use ontology created by RDBToOnto.
- The time taken for creating mapping information is not considered in D2RQ and the proposed model.

4.4 Evaluation Results

In this section, we present results of comparison evaluation of models defined in Section 4.2.
Figure 1 shows the QET. The execution time of a query is respectively similar. Therefore, QET negligibly affects the performance of the compared models.

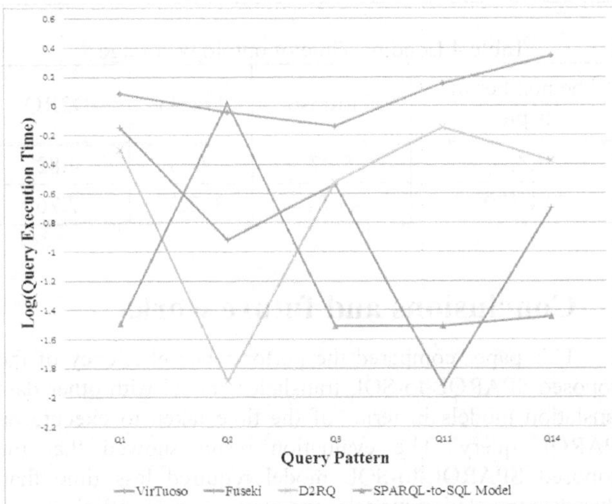

Figure 3 Query Execution Time in 714,370 triples

Tables 2 and 3 show the performance evaluation results of the proposed SPARQL-to-SQL translation model, Virtuoso, Fuseki, and D2RQ. The values in the table show TRT. As shown in the tables, the proposed SPARQL-to-SQL translation model is more efficient than other models. Virtuoso, Fuseki, and D2RQ need data loading and translation time because these models need additional ontology storage. The time it takes to convert the data stored in the RDB using RDBToOnto is 65 s for 714,370 triples and 14.27 s for 71,437 triples. In addition, these models need time to load ontology in an ontology database.

Table 4 shows the time to load ontology using Virtuoso, Fuseki, and D2RQ. Due to an increase in the number of triple loading, the time to load ontology is long. On the other hand, the proposed SPARQL-to-SQL translation model has an STT that is independent of the increase in the number of triples. Therefore, a model without additional ontology storage is more efficient than one that requires additional ontology storage.

Table 2 Total Runtime in 71,437 triples

Query Pattern	Virtuoso	Fuseki	D2RQ	Proposed
QP1	19.94	21.57	4.83	0.04
QP2	19.96	21.56	4.83	0.99
QP3	19.90	21.54	4.93	0.04
QP11	20.20	21.51	4.83	0.04
QP14	21.80	24.69	4.95	0.04

Table 3 Total Runtime in 714,370 triples

Query Pattern	Virtuoso	Fuseki	D2RQ	Proposed
QP1	114.02	429.08	8.26	0.06
QP2	113.71	428.49	7.77	1.06
QP3	113.54	428.66	8.06	0.06
QP11	114.24	428.38	8.47	0.06
QP14	115.02	428.57	8.18	0.06

Table 4 Loading Time of ontology storage

The number of triple	Virtuoso	Fuseki	D2RQ
71,437	5.07	7.23	4.82
714,370	47.81	363.37	7.76

5 Conclusions and future works

This paper compared the performance efficiency of the proposed SPARQL-to-SQL translation model with other data translation models in terms of the time taken to execute an SPARQL query. The evaluation result showed that the proposed SPARQL-to-SQL model required less time than other data translation models, and hence, is more efficient.

In future, the proposed SPARQL-to-SQL translation model will be improved to be able to support all queries provided by the LUBM for improving its performance. Further, all RDF properties must be supported through a translation algorithm. Therefore, we need to develop a more powerful translation algorithm for RDB instances.

6 Acknowledgement

This research was supported by Next-Generation Information Computing Development Program through the National Research Foundation of Korea(NRF) funded by the Ministry of Education, Science and Technology (2012M3C4A7033346). The corresponding author is Doo-Kwon Baik.

7 References

[1] Jeen Broekstra, Arjohn Kampman , Frank van Harmelen, "Sesame: A Generic Architecture for Storing and Querying RDF and RDF Schema," Springer-Verlag, Lecture Notes in Computer Science (LNCS), Vol.LNCS 2342, pp. 54-68, June 2002.

[2] Jena - A Semantic Web Framework for Java. http://jena.sourceforgee.net.

[3] http://jena.hpl.hp.com/wiki/SDB.

[4] Pan, Z. and Heflin J., "DLDB: Extending Relational Databases to Support Semantic Web Queries," InWor-kshop on Practical and Scaleable Semantic Web Systems, The Second International Semantic Webconference (ISWC2003), 2003.

[5] OWLJessKB : A Semantic Web Reasoning Tool, http://edge.cs.drexel.edu/assemblies/software/owljesskb.

[6] A. Chebotko, S. Lu, H.M. Jamil, F. Fotouhi, Semantics preserving SPARQL-to-SQL query translation for optional graph patterns, Technical Report TR-DB-052006-CLJF, Wayne State University, May 2006.

[7] S. Harris, N. Shadbolt, SPARQL query processing with conventional relational database systems, Springer-Verlag, Lecture Nodes in Computer Science. vol 3807, 2005, pp.235-244.

[8] sparql2sql – a query engine for SPARQL over Jena triple stores, http://jena.sourceforge.net/sparql2sql.

[9] F. Zemke, "Converting SPARQL to SQL," Tech. Rep., October 2006, available from http://lists.w3.org/-Archives/Public/public-rdf-dawg/2006OctDec/att-0058/sparql-to-sql.pdf.

[10] Son J, Jeong D, Baik D, "A System Model For Storage Independent Use of SPARQL-to-SQL Translation Algorithm", Journal of Korea Institute of Information Scientists and Engineers, Vol.14, Issue.5, pp.467-pp.471, 2008

[11] C Blakeley, "RDF Views of SQL Data (Declarative SQL Schema to RDF Mapping)", OpenLink Software, 2007

[12] Bizer, C., Seaborne, A. 2004. D2RQ - Treating Non-RDF Databases as Virtual RDF Graphs, In Proc of the 3rd International Semantic Web Conference.

[13] Fabrid Cerbah, Learning Highly Structured Semantic Repositories from Relational Data Databases - The RDBToOnto Tool, Proceedings of the 5th European Semantic Web Conference (ESWC 2008), Tenerife, Spain, June, 2008.

[14] Guo, Yuanbo, Zhengxiang Pan, and Jeff Heflin. "LUBM: A benchmark for OWL knowledge base systems." Web Semantics: Science, Services and Agents on the World Wide Web 3.2 (2005): 158-182.

SESSION

POSTERS AND SHORT PAPERS

Chair(s)

TBA

Modeling a Standard Health Claim Form as an RDF Store

Pavani Akundi
Cook Children's Health Care System, Fort Worth, TX, United States
Computer Science and Engineering, Southern Methodist University, Dallas, TX, United States

Abstract – *Electronic health claim forms contain nested dependencies, are highly standardized, and arranged in complex data structures. Although many organizations propose creating traditional relational databases to house these hierarchical data structures, the semantic model can also be considered as a viable alternative to the customary model. The task to convert data from a relational model to a semantic model can appear herculean; however the progressively mainstream use of the XML format can be adapted in this style of processing. The semantic data store offers an alternative maintenance model for managing data. The primary benefits include improved information processing capabilities for complex extraction, transform, and load handling. This preliminary paper presents a customizable approach to planning for and creating a semantic store for data processing.*

Keywords: RDF store, RDF/XML, semantic ontology

1 Introduction

In the healthcare industry, plan providers are constantly working with their state health agencies to process patient and insurance claim forms. The state requires strict electronic data interchange (EDI) rules and places fines on every electronic claim they reject. This places the burden of claim validation on the plan provider and clinicians to avoid costly mistakes. Providers rely on commercial services or custom software to input data directly into the electronic formats for EDI and extract, transform, and load (ETL). Both EDI and ETL are mature processes that involve many resources and complex database schemas. Yet, despite the maturity of the ongoing processes, errors occur with associated costs to the providers.

This paper proposes using semantic technologies to extract claim data and with the creation of the claim ontology to better manage the rules and structure of the extract, thus improving data validation and if successful, reduce the overhead of maintaining structural database systems and workflows.

2 Dichotomy of a Claim

There are numerous federal health claims, each with their own form and accompanying implementation guide. The 837 implementation guide is the standard for a professional or institutional medical claim and includes a rule set for generating the electronic claim for the state. The 837 implementation guide describes mandatory, optional, and situational data elements which may or may not be available on the paper claim. A database schema will be structured against these rules and the hierarchical structure the state expects.

2.1 Create an ontology

The first step in our approach will be the generation of a spreadsheet that will be the basis for deciphering the implementation guide, its hierarchy, segments, loops, and elements. Data mapping between the input source and the state repository will take place with data stored as RDF/XML. Since every claim processed by the provider will follow the same format, the schema ontology will be used to standardize claims from the RDF/XML store. Our approach includes automating semantic annotation of process models to create a planning library which contains actions and fragments [1] for every field in a database table. Ideally, every node of the model will have information processing capabilities making it an operational node [2]. In other words, the business rules for each of these nodes will be fully described in the process model library to make it very easy to generate a claim from the ontology

2.2 Convert an existing database

A relational schema for the 837 will be complex since it contains 34 loops, approximately 800 unique elements and 25 unique data types. Creating a RDF store for an existing database will support the evolution of schemas over time [3]. An RDF store is a flat file, which is portable, easy to secure, backup and maintain across applications. Compared to a relational database there will be less overhead since database software tools change often and may require resource intensive upgrades as well as deprecation of data. Large database systems and their backups required storage which can be costly to maintain. Depending on the security requirements, database systems may need to be stored on their own servers and have layers of encryption. XML's main feature is that it enables data portability by separating the presentation of the data from the content [4]. Although the general purpose of RDF/XML is to represent data on the web, it can also be a good data migration or file manipulation tool.

2.3 Conversion tools

There a several useful commercial and open source frameworks to aid in process of converting structural data and procedures into metadata. The Mulgara Semantic Store is an open source, massively scalable, transaction-safe, purpose-built database for the storage and retrieval of metadata [5]. This paper proposes using a tool similar to D2R MAP to convert a relational database to a RDF format [6] and to use Mulgara or SPARQL to extract additional relationships from the current schema tables. After an initial conversion, there may some tables or values that are not updatable and may need to be manually coded. Notation 3 (N3) is straightforward to write and the Apache Jena I/O can serialize N3 triples into RDF/XML if manual processing is necessary [7]. An exported spreadsheet of the table is good way to plan writing N3 triples which can be verified against the schema ontology.

3 Conclusions

A detailed spreadsheet has been created based on the model of the database and the next steps for this process will be to convert the file into a compatible RDF store using Jena. At this time since an online claim system to capture data entry inputs exists, our plan involves creating a process to retrieve these values and populate the schema to configure and build an electronic claim for the state. Currently, the workflow to generate a state file requires the input fields to be mapped to some middleware which will generate the file. Once the file is generated it goes through an ETL process for the state. The proposed process is a work in progress, but the creation of an RDF store/schema will serve as a proof of concept for this effort.

The conceptual model of a relational database is analogous to an ontology model such as UML. Components of the model can be mapped directly to ontology constructs [8]. The demands for healthcare applications to integrate information across systems is challenging given the use of legacy processes in parallel with modern applications. Switching to semantic processing and storage technologies is worth the cost-benefit ratio for the long term sustainability of the process. The conversion of a traditional relational database to a semantic store offers organizations a shareable and searchable database with meaningful relationships between datasets. It also offers different levels of users who need to query a system for processing beyond the claim generation and ETL process.

4 Future Work

The DBPedia knowledgebase is akin to an encyclopedia of information accessible through endpoints [9] and would be worth modeling at an infrastructure level for the health care industry. Semantic ETL methodologies and health claim form endpoints are a major contribution that would assist developers beginning the process of converting legacy systems into a semantic format. These can be appended with segment descriptions which would aid in the definition of elements as they repeat through different loops in the claim hierarchy. Health care systems look to each other to model and improve their technology patterns so the publication of common standards is a benefit to the industry.

5 References

[1] F. Lautenbacher, B. Bauer, and S. Forg, "Process mining for semantic business process modeling," in *Enterprise Distributed Object Computing Conference Workshops, 2009. EDOCW 2009. 13th*, 2009, pp. 45-53.

[2] W. Xiaoyong, Z. WeiJun, J. Tao, and Z. Yifan, "The Modeling Methodology of OIN Based on Ontology," in *Multimedia Information Networking and Security (MINES), 2011 Third International Conference on*, 2011, pp. 91-94.

[3] W3C. *Resource Description Framework (RDF)*. Available: http://www.w3.org/RDF/

[4] C. Catley and M. Frize, "Design of a health care architecture for medical data interoperability and application integration," in *Engineering in Medicine and Biology, 2002. 24th Annual Conference and the Annual Fall Meeting of the Biomedical Engineering Society EMBS/BMES Conference, 2002. Proceedings of the Second Joint*, 2002, pp. 1952-1953 vol.3.

[5] Mulgara. (March 6). *Mulgara* Available: http://www.mulgara.org/

[6] A. Szekely, A. Hejja, and R. A. Buchmann, "Mapping a Relational Database into a RDF Repository," in *Symbolic and Numeric Algorithms for Scientific Computing (SYNASC), 2011 13th International Symposium on*, 2011, pp. 175-182.

[7] A. Jena. (March 6). *Apache Jena*. Available: http://jena.apache.org/

[8] S. Zhao and E. Chang, "From Database to Semantic Web Ontology: An Overview," in *On the Move to Meaningful Internet Systems 2007: OTM 2007 Workshops*. vol. 4806, R. Meersman, Z. Tari, and P. Herrero, Eds., ed: Springer Berlin Heidelberg, 2007, pp. 1205-1214.

[9] *DBPedia*. Available: http://dbpedia.org/About

SchemaGen: A Microdata Generator for Small Business Owners

Tyronda M. Strong
Computer Science and Engineering, Southern Methodist University, Dallas, TX

Abstract – *Optimizing a website adds descriptive information in the background for search engines to read. Small business owners could benefit from a user friendly tool that would allow them to add metadata to their website without having to know HTML and XML. This metadata could increase the likelihood of the website being found in a broad based search. SchemaGen is a Java based graphical user interface that can be used to mark up data with the widely accepted and well known schema.org classes and properties. Output from the SchemaGen tool will be able to be placed on the website of the small business owner.*

Keywords: microdata, small business, schema.org, automation

1 Introduction

Small business owners (SBOs) understand the need to use marketing to get customers into the door. Using the Internet to reach more users than word of mouth or the newspaper is a tangible concept for any owner. However, the issue that most SBOs have is that they understand that search engines increase traffic but they do not know how to increase their rankings. There are three types of searches: navigational query (specific sites i.e. facebook.com), transactional query (specific tasks i.e. wells fargo in Dallas Texas), and informational query (i.e. banks in Dallas Texas). [1] Informational queries have the most benefit for a SBO because although the topic is specific it is also broad enough that an optimized website could be on the first few pages of the search results. Search engine optimization increases a website's ranking and visibility on a search engine. According to Cen and Guixing (2011), 84% of Google searchers do not go beyond the second page of the search results.[2] Search Engine optimization (SEO) is a methodology that can be implemented in various ways. Relevant keywords, links and backtracks within the website, and website structure affect the way the search engine will crawl the site and how it will rank it.[3] To solve the SBO's annotation problem, we created the SchemaGen Tool.

2 Methodology

2.1 Microdata and Schema.org

Our methodology for building this tool utilizes microdata and schema.org. HTML5 introduced the concept of microdata which "enables you to specify machine-readable custom elements in a web page by using syntax made up of name-value pairs with existing content". [4] Google, Bing, Yahoo, and Yandex created their own vocabulary of name-value pairs called schema.org. [5] Marking up the content on a website allows the user to speak the language of the major search engines. Since most SBO's are not proficient in marking up the HTML on their website into RDF/XML (Resource Description Framework which describes information on the Internet) [6] or microdata, the SchemaGen tool was created to fill the gap. This tool allows the user to utilize semantic web technologies without having to know the specifics in writing ontologies, RDF/XML, or triples. Using schema.org instead of creating a site specific ontology will make the information more streamlined with what the search engine recognizes versus a smaller, less well known ontology.

2.2 SchemaGen

The SchemaGen Tool was created for users who have a little knowledge of semantic web and microdata. Using Java and the Jena framework, which reads, processes, and writes RDF data, [7] the tool allows a user to add metadata based on the classes and properties in schema.org to annotate their data. Schema.org has created high level classes for many categories of data found on the web. Each class aims to give the webmaster enough attributes that the class can be fully explained to the search engine and return meaningful data to the user. Currently, the user places their web page content in the tool and uses menus and drop-downs to select the attributes that best describe the highlighted content. The output is an RDF/XML file that can be merged with HTML source on a webpage.

3 Conclusions

Utilizing the vocabulary developed by the major search engines and semi-automating the markup process with the SchemaGen tool allows SBOs to optimize their website for the search engines. We plan to measure the increase of visibility after SchemaGen is deployed. In the next iteration of the SchemaGen tool, it will parse well-formed HTML and generate the microdata for the user instead of a RDF/XML file.

4 References

[1] Weller, B., and Calcott, L.: 'Marketing with AdWords': 'The Definitive Guide to Google AdWords' (Apress, 2012), pp. 39-62

[2] Cen, Z., and Guixing, W.: 'Research and Analysis of Search Engine Optimization Factors Based on Reverse Engineeing', in Editor (Ed.)^(Eds.): 'Book Research and Analysis of Search Engine Optimization Factors Based on Reverse Engineeing' (2011, edn.), pp. 225-228

[3] Fuxue, W., Yi, L., and Yiwen, Z.: 'An empirical study on the search engine optimization technique and its outcomes', in Editor (Ed.)^(Eds.): 'Book An empirical study on the search engine optimization technique and its outcomes' (2011, edn.), pp. 2767-2770

[4] Casario, M., Elst, P., Brown, C., Wormser, N., and Hanquez, C.: 'HTML5 Structural and Semantic Elements': 'HTML5 Solutions: Essential Techniques for HTML5 Developers' (Apress, 2011), pp. 31-61

[5] http://semanticweb.com/google-yahoo-and-bing-announce-schema-org_b20301, accessed July 12 2012

[6] http://www.w3.org/TR/2004/REC-rdf-concepts-20040210/#section-Introduction, accessed March 8 2013

[7] http://jena.apache.org/, accessed March 10 2013

SESSION

BIOINFORMATICS

Chair(s)

TBA

RESTful API in life science research systems and data integration challenges: linking metabolic pathway, metabolic network, gene and publication.

Etienne Z. Gnimpieba, Brent S. Anderson, Carol M. Lushbough
Computer Science Department, University of South Dakota, 414 E. Clark St. Vermillion, SD 57069, USA,
{Etienne.gnimpieba; Brent.Anderson ; Carol.Lushbough}@usd.edu

Corresponding author: Etienne.gnimpieba@usd.edu, +1 605 223 0383.

~o~

Abstract: Translational science research development requires life sciences researchers to update their concept on systems integration and data integration. The RESTful API has proven to be very useful in integrating the massive amount of data and tools. This work presents an approach for biological systems analysis based on the semantic web and RESTful API. The integration of this approach in the BioExtract Server engine as a Workflow Management System (WMS) allows us to apply our work to the linking of several biological levels (metabolic pathway, metabolic network model, genes and publications).

Keywords: Systems Biology, Bioinformatics, RESTful API, BioExtract Server, Data Integration, Systems Integration.

1. Introduction

With the democratization of the Internet and the advent of web 3.0, the databases in the life sciences fields have grown exponentially. Given this data accumulation, new technologies for data representations are used (ontologies, big data technologies) [1] with tools being created at a frantic pace [2][3]. In this rat race, biological issues evolve slower. Although the formulations change, the biologist is always seeking answers to simple research hypotheses. In this gigantic labyrinth, the advent of Semantic Web tools using the RESTful API makes a substantial contribution [4]. This work presents an application of this technology for the systems and data integration in life science at several levels (genetic, enzymatic, metabolic) with references related to these data (publications).

2. All systems go: Systems Biology and Biological Systems challenges

Science evolves its methods too. For a simple biological question on gene g related to the development of a given disease D, an answer involves the influence of different biological levels (gene, RNA, protein, metabolite, transcription factor, environmental factor, etc.), thus involving data from several life sciences areas (genetics, genomics, proteomics, transcriptomics, metabolomics, epidemiology, etc.) [5][6] (Figure 1). This involvement is not new in itself, but previous scientific methods did not allow easy integration into the response to the biological question. With the advent of systems biology, it is now possible to cross data from several fields using systems and data integration [2], [7–10]. Once the systems and data are integrated, we obtain a massive infrastructure (Big Systems) and a huge amount of data (Big Data). Managing this data using RESTful API is very effective[11].

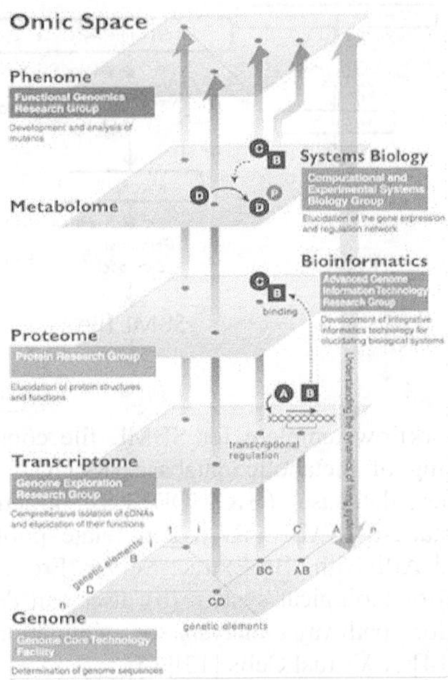

Figure 1: Example in life science domains inter-dependence, Systems Biology and Bioinformatics used. [6].

3. BioExtract Server engine: RESTful API-based Workflow Management Systems (WMS)

BioExtract Server is a semantic web based (ontology, WSDL. SOAP, RESTful API) WMS engine. This engine offers an opportunity to connect to multiple data sources, extract data in several formats, load data and use data management tools to manipulate them. The more interesting feature in this tool is its ability to allows a user to record each chosen step in a work data management process (Extract Load and Treat, ELT) for reuse or sharing with other users. This process is recorded in the workflow as an XML file[12] (Figure 2).

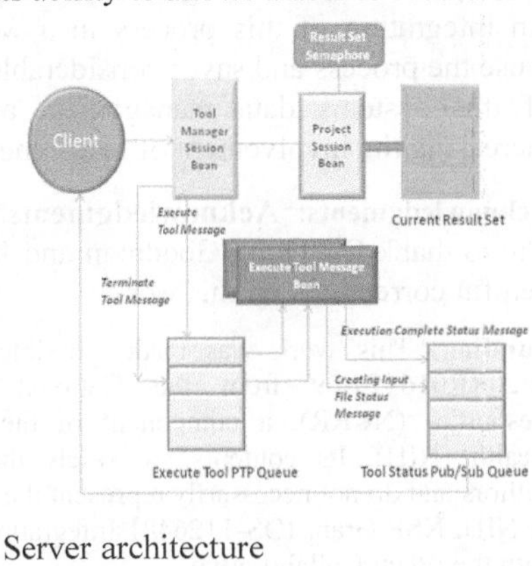

Figure 2: BioExtract Server architecture

4. Use case: using workflow for linking metabolic pathway, metabolic network model, gene list and publication.

Using the RESTful API, we integrated several database into the BioExtract Server: KEGG for metabolic pathway, enzyme and gene, BioModels for metabolic network model and ontology annotation data, BRENDA for enzyme kinetics and reactions parameters descriptions, and SABIO-RK for pathways related to reaction kinetics parameter value. This integration allows us to design several workflow templates integrating data from each database in a validated Systems Biology Markup Language (SBML) file construction (Figures 3).

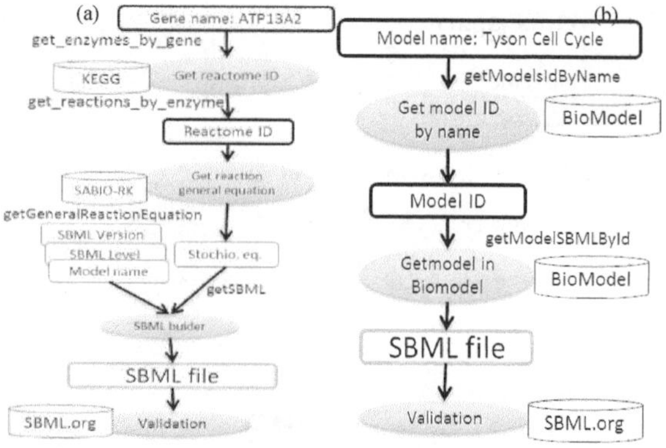

Figures 3: workflow template for SBML file construction from the linking of metabolic database (KEGG), Systems Biology model database (BIOMODELS), kinetics and parameters database (SABIO-RK), and relate publications using RESTful API with BioExtract Server. From a given gene name (a) or biological system (b), user can design an SBML file for pathway analysis or simulation using FBASimVis [14] or Virtual Cells [13][15].

5. Conclusion

RESTful APIs-based tools are very useful, especially for managing massive data from different data sources. The integration of the API in a WMS such as BioExtract Server allows the manipulation of huge and complex data in a personalized way that avoids complexity, reduces errors and supports sharability. We show here two examples of how a biologist can extract data on metabolic networks (metabolic pathway, metabolic network model, gene) and publications relating to this data, using a simple integrated user interface. An integration of this process in a workflow allows us to reuse the process and saves considerable time. The effeteness of this systems data management approach depends on increasing the involvement of researchers.

Acknowledgments: **Acknowledgments**: The authors would like to thank Dr. Doug Goodman and Jerry Prentice for their helpful corrections on this work.

Funding: This work was made possible by SD-INBRE Grant #P20RR016479-09 from the National Center for Research Resources (NCRR), a component of the National Institutes of Health (NIH). Its contents are solely the responsibility of the authors and do not necessarily represent the official views of NCRR or NIH. NSF Grant IOS-1126481 Integrating the BioExtract Server with the iPlant Collaborative.

References

[1] Z. Zhang, K.-H. Cheung, and J. P. Townsend, "Bringing Web 2.0 to bioinformatics.," Briefings in bioinformatics, vol. 10, no. 1, pp. 1–10, Jan. 2009.

[2] "All systems go.," Nature, vol. 439, no. 7073, pp. 136–7, Jan. 2006.

[3] O. Wolkenhauer, C. Auffray, R. Jaster, G. Steinhoff, and O. Dammann, "The road from systems biology to systems medicine.," Pediatric research, Jan. 2013.

[4] C. M. Lushbough, D. M. Jennewein, and V. P. Brendel, "The BioExtract Server: a web-based bioinformatic workflow platform.," Nucleic acids research, vol. 39, no. Web Server issue, pp. W528–32, Jul. 2011.

[5] D. Hwang, A. G. Rust, S. Ramsey, J. J. Smith, D. M. Leslie, A. D. Weston, P. de Atauri, J. D. Aitchison, L. Hood, A. F. Siegel, and H. Bolouri, "A data integration methodology for systems biology.," Proceedings of the National Academy of Sciences of the United States of America, vol. 102, no. 48, pp. 17296–301, Nov. 2005.

[6] T. Toyoda, Y. Mochizuki, K. Player, N. Heida, N. Kobayashi, and Y. Sakaki, "OmicBrowse: a browser of multidimensional omics annotations.," Bioinformatics (Oxford, England), vol. 23, no. 4, pp. 524–6, Mar. 2007.

[7] P. Kersey and R. Apweiler, "Linking publication, gene and protein data.," Nature cell biology, vol. 8, no. 11, pp. 1183–9, Nov. 2006.

[8] A. Carlier, L. Geris, K. Bentley, G. Carmeliet, P. Carmeliet, and H. Van Oosterwyck, "MOSAIC: a multiscale model of osteogenesis and sprouting angiogenesis with lateral inhibition of endothelial cells.," PLoS computational biology, vol. 8, no. 10, p. e1002724, Jan. 2012.

[9] W. Zhang, F. Li, and L. Nie, "Integrating multiple 'omics' analysis for microbial biology: application and methodologies.," Microbiology (Reading, England), vol. 156, no. Pt 2, pp. 287–301, Feb. 2010.

[10] A. Harel, I. Dalah, S. Pietrokovski, and M. Safran, "Bioinformatics for Omics Data," Data Management, vol. 719, pp. 71–96, 2011.

[11] C. Lushbough, M. K. Bergman, C. J. Lawrence, D. Jennewein, and V. Brendel, "BioExtract server--an integrated workflow-enabling system to access and analyze heterogeneous, distributed biomolecular data.," IEEE/ACM transactions on computational biology and bioinformatics / IEEE, ACM, vol. 7, no. 1, pp. 12–24.

[12] C. M. Lushbough and V. P. Brendel, "An overview of the BioExtract Server: a distributed, Web-based system for genomic analysis.," Advances in experimental medicine and biology, vol. 680, pp. 361–9, Jan. 2010.

[13] J. Fisher and T. A. Henzinger, "Executable cell biology.," Nature biotechnology, vol. 25, no. 11, pp. 1239–49, Nov. 2007.

[14] E. Grafahrend-Belau, C. Klukas, B. H. Junker, and F. Schreiber, "FBA-SimVis: interactive visualization of constraint-based metabolic models.," Bioinformatics (Oxford, England), vol. 25, no. 20, pp. 2755–7, Oct. 2009.

[15] I. I. Moraru, J. C. Schaff, B. M. Slepchenko, and L. M. Loew, "The virtual cell: an integrated modeling environment for experimental and computational cell biology.," Annals of the New York Academy of Sciences, vol. 971, pp. 595–6, Oct. 2002.